IMAGINATIVE GARDENING

DAVID STEVENS

MARTIN BOOKS

Published by Martin Books
Simon & Schuster International Group
Fitzwilliam House
32 Trumpington Street
Cambridge CB2 1QY

in association with B&Q plc
Portswood House
1 Hampshire Corporate Park
Chandlers Ford
Eastleigh
Hants SO5 3YX

First published 1990

ISBN 0 85941 619 4

Text © B&Q plc; illustrations © Woodhead-Faulkner (Publishers) Ltd, 1990
Copyright in photographs belongs to individual owners, detailed below

B&Q gardens
Some photographs in this book show B&Q's Chelsea Flower Show gardens.
These are on page 9 (1987); pages 17, 67 and 68 (1988, Gold Medal); and
page 130 (1989, Gold Medal/'Sword of Excellence').

Design: Andrew Shoolbred
Illustrations: Peter Bull, Ann Baum and David Stevens
Typesetting: Pentacor PLC, High Wycombe, Bucks
Origination: Adroit Photo Litho Ltd, Birmingham
Printed and bound in Spain by Graficas Estella, SA

Acknowledgements
The publishers, author and B&Q plc would like to thank the following
individuals and companies for permission to reproduce photographs:

   The Garden Picture Library – Wolfram Stehling (front cover)
   S&O Mathews Photography (pages 12; 31; 88; 89; 95; 96)
   Bob Gibbons/Natural Image (pages 16; 32; 61, except top right; 133)
   Liz Gibbons/Natural Image (pages 25; 35; 46; 78)
   Pictor International – London (pages 26, below; 43; 52; 73, both; 87; 90;
      98, left)
   Robert Harding Picture Library (pages 116; 128)
   Photos Horticultural Picture Library (pages 134 and back cover)
   Ibstock Building Products Ltd (page 61, top right)

All other photographs provided by the author or B&Q plc

CONTENTS

THE AUTHOR

David Stevens has been B&Q's Gardening Consultant since 1987. As well as advising them on horticultural matters he designs B&Q's show gardens for the Chelsea Flower Show each year.

David is Managing Director of Individual Gardens Limited, which offers a total design and building package to both developers and the public. Individual Gardens pioneered the concept of the 'fitted garden' and is almost certainly the largest design practice in Europe, creating gardens for national magazines, house developers and private clients in every walk of life.

David has worked in gardening and landscaping since 1969. He trained at Thames Polytechnic and after working as landscape designer at Syon Park, went on to form a private practice, becoming landscape consultant to *Homes and Gardens,* and setting up their garden planning service. In 1972, his first garden at the Chelsea Flower Show won the Banksian Silver Gilt Medal. Since then he has won a total of twelve awards at Chelsea, including seven gold medals and the Wilkinson Sword Trophy in 1989 for the best garden in the show.

David has written seven books on garden design, including *Creative Gardening* (Hamlyn); his latest title is *Town Gardens* (Conran Octopus). He contributes regularly to gardening magazines and national newspapers. Listeners to many radio programmes, including 'Woman's Hour', 'You and Yours' and a number of local radio shows have benefited from David's wisdom; he has also appeared on the BBC's 'Gardener's World' and has been co-presenter of TVS's 'That's Gardening' over several series.

A Founder Member and elected Fellow of the Society of Landscape and Garden Designers, David is a full member of the Institute of Horticulture, a consultant to the Royal National Rose Society and a member of the Royal Horticultural Society Gardens subcommittee.

Home for David is in Buckingham, where he lives in a Victorian town house with a long, narrow garden. The Stevens family spend as much time as they can in their 'outside room', and the garden has been designed by David for minimum maintenance and maximum enjoyment – the principles he explains in this book.

INTRODUCTION

The way in which we think about gardens and gardening is rapidly changing. No longer are gardens places in which to dig, stake and tie in a laborious cycle! They are instead becoming an extension of the house and a valuable 'outside room' that should seek to accommodate your family's way of life.

The trouble is that many people shy away from the whole idea of garden-design and construction; they feel it will be too difficult or too expensive, when in fact it should be the simplest solution to their own particular set of requirements. Professionals do not, as many people think, conjure ideas out of thin air. They may from time to time be inspired to create something very special, but on the whole they work to a tried and tested set of rules that they know will produce a satisfactory result.

This means that an effective garden is planned in logical stages: finding out what you have; asking what you need; and subsequently evolving a basic plan. Into this can be woven the preparation of the site; the use of hard and soft surfaces; the importance of planting in both visual and practical terms; and finally the benefits of features and furnishings that bring the whole 'composition' to life.

Of course, the problems are not always straightforward; many gardens are awkward shapes, have difficult slopes or lack privacy, and so need to be tackled in a specific way. It is also true to say that there is so great a choice of plants and equipment available from mail-order catalogues, nurseries and garden centres that you can become totally confused. It is little wonder that many gardens end up as a jumble of unrelated features, with high maintenance requirements! Over-complication is the opposite of good design, and I have set out in this book to show you how to get the best from your plot, at the same time letting it reflect you and your needs.

Remember that it is *you* who makes your garden unique, so never slavishly copy ideas — from this or any other book. Gain inspiration by all means, seek ideas certainly, but, in the final analysis, create something that is just right for *you,* and your family.

Sound garden-planning makes sense. It allows you to carry out construction over an extended period, enables you to obtain competitive quotes should you need them, and, most importantly, gives you a valuable extra room that can cater for a wide range of activities.

A garden can be as little or as much work as you want; it can be a hobby or a simple open space. What it should never be is a burden, for as soon as you become a slave to that room outside then it no longer fulfils its purpose.

Enjoyment is the all-important key, and enjoyable gardens are not difficult to plan and construct. This book tells you how to go about it, and I know from experience that garden-planning and construction not only work but are a lot of fun to do.

GETTING STARTED

Why design a garden?

To start any project without having some firm ideas about the end result usually spells disaster, and, unfortunately, this is nowhere more true than in the garden.

In many ways, it is easy to see why so many plots end up as an unco-ordinated jumble of features, because in most instances the rooms inside the house have to take first priority, particularly when the owners have just moved into a brand-new home. Such a garden usually grows out of desperation rather than according to any set plan, and features like paving, patio, lawn, planting and buildings are incorporated when pressure from the household demands them. Such a course of action not only lacks cohesion, but almost inevitably costs far more than necessary, works poorly in visual and practical terms and can lead to high levels of maintenance, none of which is desirable!

Many people think that they have to be 'gardeners' to succeed in either planning a layout or growing things successfully; in fact nothing could be further from the truth. A good garden that works for you is based largely on common sense and wholly on simplicity.

Your personality governs how your garden will look and work. Three plots next door to one another will turn out quite differently, not because of any inequalities in shape, aspect, slope or soil but because different families have different circumstances. These might range from moving into a brand-new home with a moonscape for a garden to moving into an older property with an established plot that needs modification. You might want to make the garden easier to manage, or change it as the family grows up. Most likely of all you will be tired of looking at a motley collection of old sheds, dustbins, washing line and poorly-laid surfaces. Although a garden has to contain the ugly as well as the beautiful, remember that all these important items can be organised in such a way as to enhance rather than detract from the overall composition.

Assessing what you have

We have just seen that there are many reasons for planning a garden. As an experienced designer I have worked on projects from gardens that covered many acres right down to tiny courtyards. Although these have obviously widely different requirements, the way in which I go about planning them remains essentially the same. It revolves around the two basic questions of 'what do you have?' and 'what do you want?'.

Rather than jotting down ideas and facts at random we use simple check-lists (page 8), which not only ensure that you leave nothing out, but also help to clarify your ideas, and the way in which you think about your garden as a whole.

Any good garden plan takes these questions in

A well planned garden can be an 'outdoor room' for the whole family.

sequence. The first involves you in a simple survey, and also asks you to look at your plot in rather more detail, so that you understand not only its advantages and limitations, but also the immediate surroundings that will bear on the finished composition.

Measuring the garden
Many people think that a survey is something to do with men in yellow helmets carrying theodolites and ranging rods, and so is quite beyond the average gardener. Forget it! All you need is a long tape measure (30 m or 100 foot), a clean pad of paper, a clip board, a pencil and a few bamboo canes, easily bought from any garden centre. Never try and measure a garden without such basic equipment. The fact that many gardens are planned on the back of envelopes simply ensures

What do you have?

Northpoint	☐
Changes in level	☐
Good or bad views	☐
Position of doors/windows	☐
Position of garage	☐
Soil type: acid/alkaline/light/heavy	☐
Existing trees/plants	☐
Manholes	☐
Existing paved areas	☐
(including type)_____	

What do you want?

Terrace/patio	☐	Swings/slide	☐
Summerhouse	☐	Herb bed	☐
Rockery	☐	Fruit trees	☐
Built-in barbecue	☐	Veg plot large/small	☐
Bin screen	☐	Shed	☐
Play area	☐	Rockery with stream	☐
Soft fruit	☐	Arbour	☐
Roses	☐	Sandpit	☐
Lawn	☐	Washing line	☐
Greenhouse	☐	(type)_____	
Pond/pool	☐		
Pergola	☐	Annuals	☐
Dog run	☐	Herbaceous	☐

Anything else you would like?
(Special features or effects you would like, favourite plants, colours, etc.)
_____
_____
_____

Anything you don't want?
_____
_____
_____

Anything about yourself and family?

Are you a keen gardener	☐
Average gardener	☐
Lazy gardener	☐
Ages of children?_____	
Any pets?_____	
What will your garden be mainly used for?_____	

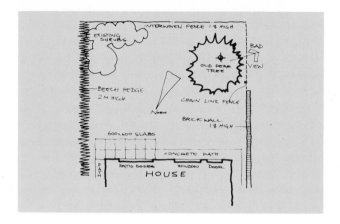

Start by sketching the outline of your house and garden.

Once this is done, take your first measurement across the back of the house, by anchoring the tape with a cane against one boundary and running it right the way across to the other side. Now read off the measurements in order, noting down the edge of the house, both sides of windows and doors, and the position of any drains, manholes and so on. Once you have measured across the space, do exactly the same thing down the garden, checking edges of existing paving, lawn, trees and so on. If the tape does not reach all the way down the plot, mark the end with a cane, reel the tape in and start from where you left off; clearly mark this 'change point' on your plan as well.

failure as the end result; it is sad that many so-called professional landscape gardeners still work in this way.

Start off by going outside and drawing the outline of your house, roughly, freehand. Clearly show doors and windows. Mark the position and approximate line of the garden's boundaries, noting what they are made of, for example brick wall, fence, deciduous or evergreen hedge, wire strands and so on. Also note any other features such as trees, planting, buildings, walls and changes in level. Don't leave anything out at this stage, even if you are sure you want to be rid of it. It is amazing how often a poorly shaped tree can be pruned into shape, an old shrubbery revived, or an unkempt hedge that straddles the area become an important part of the design later on.

Remember that certain plants, namely hardy perennials, die down during the winter months and will not be visible. If you carry out a survey at this time of the year it can be well worth checking planted areas again in the spring, to see if any new material has shown its head above ground.

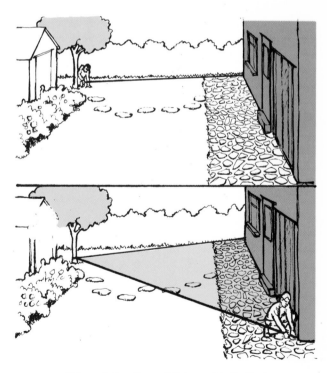

Triangulation (page 10) is used to fix the position of trees and angled boundaries.

If the garden is a straightforward rectangle, with little in the way of trees or other features, this first stage is very simple. If, however, the plot is an awkward shape, or trees are positioned in such a way as to make 'running measurements' difficult, you may have to undertake the simple job of 'triangulation'.

This involves running a tape from two known points to the object in question. To find a tree in this way, you might run the tape from one corner of the house and note down the distance, and then move the tape to another known point – the other side of the house or perhaps the corner of a garage – and take another measurement (see illustrations below). This will 'fix' the tree

firmly on the survey and when you come to draw the plan to scale you can transfer the measurement. You will find a detailed description of how to do this on pages 15–16. Use the same technique for finding the junction of two angled boundaries.

Changes in level

If a garden has so many cross falls (slopes across the garden) and steep slopes that it is impossible for you to carry out reasonably accurate measurements, or if the site is 'dog-legged' or has many trees, it may well be worth enlisting the services of a qualified surveyor. His fees will be well worth it and you will be safe in the knowledge that you have a sound starting point for your design.

In most circumstances, you can work out the slopes easily enough, simply by sighting back to the house and measuring the drop with a tape. If there are existing retaining walls (walls that sup-

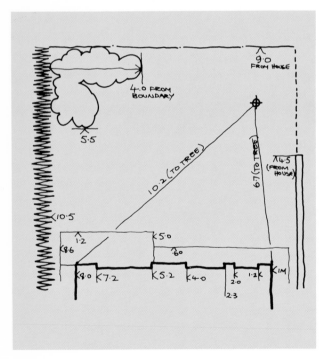

Add running measurements and triangulation measurements as you go along

Measuring level changes in the garden – sight back to the house and measure with a tape.

port an upper level), a course of brick usually equals 7.5 cm (3 inches).

If you are moving into a new house, and its survey drawings are available, check they are accurate before using them. Very often levels may have been adjusted or houses set at different heights to those originally indicated.

Up to now, we have been concerned with the physical dimensions of the site, but there are a number of other factors to survey that may well influence the finished garden.

Views

All gardens have views, even if they are completely hemmed in by high city walls. Such views can be good or bad and may need to be emphasised or screened accordingly.

In positive terms, a good view can be a priceless part of your design and will need to be highlighted in some way. This may mean creating a gap to frame a view through a hedge or planting, or doing quite the opposite in an empty site by drawing the eye in a particular direction. Remember that a wide-open view is often less effective than one that is gently highlighted by carefully positioned plants and features, as shown in the photograph overleaf.

Rather more frequently, particularly in urban or suburban areas, the outlook is less promising. Here there will be a need for screening, either with walls, or fences, or again with areas of planting. In town, there is often the problem of being overlooked by neighbours' windows, and so a well positioned tree or pergola, or overhead beams run out from the house, may be useful to break the offending sight-line.

Whether a view is good or bad, make a note of it on your survey and mark the approximate angle from your main viewing points both inside and outside the house.

Shelter

It is a fact that lack of shelter, rather than temperature, is the main reason for not using a garden to the full. In virtually every situation there is a prevailing wind or persistent turbulence set up by neighbouring buildings, walls and tree groups. Make a note of this, together with the direction from which the problem usually arises. Wind that blows at an angle against a wall tends to accelerate; wind hitting a solid surface head-on turns under upon itself, and creates unpleasant conditions for people and plants alike. The erection of a solid wind-break only tends to create greater turbulence; the answer is either to position a screen of tough plants to help filter the wind and reduce its force, or to erect a slatted fence that does much the same thing but takes up rather less room.

Check whether the garden has either a 'rain shadow' (page 111) or a 'frost hollow' (page 84), and decide whether these could be eliminated.

Soil

The soil that surrounds a house is of vital importance, as it is this that will determine what you can and cannot grow. It is built up from two basic layers: *topsoil*, which is fertile, containing nutrients, bacteria and insects; and *subsoil*, which is, for growing purposes, virtually dead. Topsoil should be just that, and to support healthy vigorous growth you should have 23–30 cm (9–12 inches) of it. Unfortunately, on many new building sites the topsoil is either buried beneath a layer of infertile subsoil or missing altogether. To try and improve subsoil is almost impossible, and it is best to get rid of it, by importing topsoil to take its place; remove subsoil if necessary, depending on existing levels. If you do move into a new home, you have a perfect right to ensure that the developer does this for you.

Garden features can be planned to provide a frame that makes the most of a fine view.

Sometimes topsoil has been heavily compacted, leading to poor drainage and limiting root development. If this is the case, deep rotovating – with a mechanical digger, available from a hire shop – normally resolves the problem.

Any soil will have a tendency to be either acid or alkaline, and this will dictate the type of plants that will flourish. If the surrounding area is chalky or has deposits of limestone, the soil will probably be alkaline; if it is rich in organic matter, and peat in particular, it will lean towards acidity. To check your soil, use a simple kit available from most good garden centres; take samples from several places, as the readings can vary considerably. Soils at the extreme ends of the range can be countered with careful applications of lime for acidity, and peat or a fertiliser called 'sequestrene' for chalky conditions.

In most cases, it makes sense to work with what you have; it is virtually impossible to change a basic soil type, particularly in the longer term. Use plants that flourish in your particular type of soil; they will be happier and so will you!

The water-table
This is the level that water naturally finds in the ground. It generally rises and falls in response to rain, but can also be affected by earth-moving or a lot of new building. A high water-table and excessively damp ground can stunt plant growth and make digging difficult. Conversely, a lack of water starves plants of the nutrients vital to healthy development. Irrigation can cure the latter, but to lower a high water-table, drainage may be necessary. This is explained more fully on pages 33-5.

Sun and shade
The most important piece of survey information I have left to last. The north point, or where the sun shines throughout the day, largely dictates just how the garden design is prepared. Certain plants and features need specific conditions: ponds and patios like to be in the sun, as do greenhouses, vegetables and play areas; other plants will enjoy shade, and so will the compost heap! The relative height of the sun varies from summer to winter and this will affect the length of shadow cast by trees and buildings, so take this into account. It can be useful to show the passage of the sun throughout the day with an arc on your survey, starting on one side (the east) and setting on the other (the west).

Deciding what you want

By carrying out a survey you have not only been able to note what you have inside and outside those garden boundaries, but, almost as important, you should now have a 'feel' for your outside

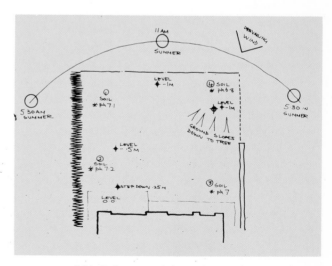

Add all the survey information you have collected to your rough sketch.

room; you know its characteristics, and its good and bad points.

Even though you may be getting some positive ideas of just what you want to see in the garden, resist the urge to start planning right away; the important job now is to crystallise your thoughts.

Draw up a list of what you want, and don't forget to throw this open to the whole family; children may well be using the space more than you. Take your time and try to include everything. It does not matter at this stage if the list seems endless; you can always thin it down later! The important thing is not to leave anything out. It can be very difficult to add a forgotten feature once the garden is finished, and it inevitably looks like an afterthought, as well as involving unnecessary expense.

A list for an average family – if there is such a thing! – might include: a patio of ample size for sitting, dining and play; a barbecue; raised beds; a lawn; borders; screening; shelter; a water feature; a pergola; play equipment; a swing; a slide; a shed; a greenhouse; a compost heap; an incinerator; a washing line; dustbins and so on. Some garden features may be far more dominant than others: room to park a boat, or wash the car, or for a large rockery or pool, for instance. These may well be the pivot of the entire garden, and they will need to be looked at in these terms later.

As well as making this list, ask yourself several other questions. Am I a keen, average or lazy gardener, and in consequence how much time am I likely to spend on maintenance? How much money am I prepared to invest? Remember it will be an investment, because a well planned garden often realises its full cost and more when you come to sell. While on this point, make sure you allocate a sensible budget. Garden materials, plants and equipment are excellent value, but, like everything else, their cost in hard cash mounts up.

Most important of all, ask if there is anything a member of the family positively dislikes. This is something a lot of people forget, particularly when it comes to planning the planting layout of the garden.

The answers to all the questions really are important and it is far better to design and implement a straightforward scheme that you can afford than a grand composition that will make impossible demands on your energy, time, and, perhaps most important of all, your pocket.

A good garden-plan will save your hard-earned cash, because you will only have to buy what you really want, rather than trying to incorporate random purchases that seemed a good idea at the time. A sensible design will also allow you to build the garden over a period of time, easing the pressure on funds.

DESIGN

Many people are wary of 'design' and 'designers', feeling that the whole subject is something of a mystery. Glossy books and magazines crammed full of sumptuous interiors and impeccably manicured 'designer' gardens only compound the problem, and it is little wonder that most of us feel that such grand compositions are beyond us. The truth of the matter is that, on the whole, they are! But this is no reason why good design should not be just as applicable to a small backyard as to an estate of many acres.

Neither should this word 'design' have any mystery about it; it simply means that one should employ sensible criteria to solve a straightforward problem, something that designers achieve every working day by following a logical set of rules. There are, of course, various factors that influence the way the job is tackled and the eventual outcome, and, as we have already seen, *personality* is a key factor in all this.

In other words, your personality will mould the finished garden, as will all the information that you gathered during the initial survey. The time you spent in fact-finding may have seemed frustrating, but it has already gone a long way to setting the theme, and allowing you to embark on an exciting project: the creation of a new environment for all the family. Before you can begin formulating your ideas, however, you need to do two things. First you must make a scale drawing of your garden so that you have a framework in which to design. Secondly, before you start doing anything on paper you have to ask yourself some important questions about the type of garden you want.

Preparing a scale drawing

To do this accurately is important, for if the drawing is not correctly to scale it will be impossible to position and locate features properly, and in consequence the proportions of the garden when built would be incorrect. The easiest way to work is over a sheet of graph paper, selecting a simple scale of so many squares to the metre or foot. In a garden of average size, a scale of 1:100 (1 cm:1 m *or* ⅛ inch:1 foot) will be suitable, fitting easily onto an A3 sheet of paper; for a smaller garden or back yard a scale of 1:50 (2 cm:1 m *or* ¼ inch:1 foot) would be better.

Stick the sheet of graph paper down to a clean, smooth surface with drafting tape or sellotape, and place a sheet of tracing paper over it, attaching the tracing paper in a similar way. Using a pencil, transfer the running measurements from your survey drawing on to the graph paper, and you will see that the position and shape of the house, boundaries, planting and other features soon take shape.

If finding a tree or other feature involved triangulation, transfer it on to the drawing in the following way. Locate one of the two positions you took measurements to the object from. Extend a

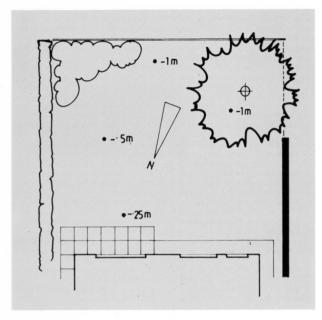

Make an accurate scale drawing from your sketch and transfer all the survey information.

pair of compasses to the (scaled) distance shown on your survey and put one arm on the known point, and draw an arc. Repeat the exercise from the second point in exactly the same way; where the arcs intersect is the exact position of the object you wish to find.

Once all the measurements have been transferred, make a note of the other factors we discussed earlier. The prevailing wind, good or bad views, the types of boundary, existing features, changes of level, and, of course, that all-important north point.

Once your scale drawing is finished, take half-a-dozen photocopies on which you can formulate the actual design, and file away both the original and the survey drawing for safe-keeping.

Before you begin putting any of your thoughts on to paper, you have to ask yourself what the limitations of size, shape and locality on your garden are, and consider what sort of 'feel' you want your garden to have.

Local style

Style is a much misunderstood idea; most people simply confuse it with fashion, which is something altogether different and more transient. When talking of style in terms of garden design, the primary aim is to create a composition that respects local traditions in materials and which is in keeping with the surrounding landscape. The all-too-common incongruity of Westmorland rockery stone used in a suburban Surrey garden, or Cotswold walling used in Cumbria, should be self-evident. They are far from home, and look it. Add to this the high cost of transporting such materials around the country and the whole idea begins to look decidedly suspect! To use such fine materials in this way may be fashionable but it has little to do with good design; it's a waste of

Even a tiny city garden can be designed to maximise its potential as a living area.

the natural beauty of such materials to misuse them in such a fashion.

Taking the idea of affinities a stage further: one would not immediately think of using a crisp timber deck, brightly coloured awnings and a plastic lawn outside a fine period building, although such materials might be more than valid on a roof garden in the centre of town.

Of course, these are extreme examples, and most of us live in rather simpler situations, perhaps on a new development of houses or in the suburbs of a city. Here the choices may seem rather less clear, but even so there is often a theme or range of materials that you can use.

House blends into garden as overhead beams combine height and an architectural line.

The stone used on this patio matches the house, and creates a harmonious look.

Linking house and garden

Ideally, house and garden should work as a single unit, with a smooth transition between inside and out. A perfect example of this arises when the effect of a fine old farmhouse floor, laid in mellow stone, is repeated using similar stone flags for the terrace just outside. This is an unusual and, incidentally, expensive solution, but it underlines the point that it can pay dividends in visual terms to respect local building materials and traditions.

On a more mundane level, many houses are brick-built: what could be more natural than using a similar brick, teamed with, say, a neat pre-cast slab, on the patio outside the sliding glass doors? Another link would be to use a fine collection of house plants on one side of those doors with a corresponding shrub bed on the other.

In town gardens, the division between plots, at least close to the house, is often marked with a brick or block wall. This is an ideal opportunity to extend a colour scheme from the interior out into the garden along the wall in question. Back this up with plants that display similar flower or leaf colour for an even better effect. Remember that such plants may also give you the benefit of their perfume, as well as the whisper of foliage in a gentle breeze. Gardens should never be thought of in simply visual terms but offer the chance to appeal to the senses of touch, smell and hearing. The patio doors give you not only access and a view, but all these other advantages too.

But what of a house that has little to offer in terms of its construction materials, a simply rendered building perhaps? Well, here you have a free hand to use whatever you like, as long as you

Rectangular, architectural lines at all levels near the house link house and garden.

remember that complication spells disaster and simplicity wins every time. Bricks, slabs, timber decking, brushed concrete or even railway sleepers can all be used as paving. All might be ideal and we will look at all of them in greater detail later on.

One final point is to do with scale: you need to think of correcting the inequality of height between the obvious bulk of the building and the flatter plane of the garden outside. This you can start to achieve close to the house with raised beds, walling, built-in seating and sculptural planting. Overhead beams that run out from the building not only extend a naturally architectural line, but, when clothed with fragrant climbers, cast a light shade. They may also be useful in breaking the sight-line of windows in an adjoining property. The photograph on page 17 is a good example of their use in this way. Further away, trees, garden buildings, pergolas and bolder shrubs will play their part, all helping that vital link between house and garden.

Usually the house is the starting point for a garden design. It makes sense to make the area immediately adjacent to the house relatively 'architectural', to link with the clean lines of the building. The further away you get, the softer and looser the design can become, so that towards the bottom of the garden one can be working in strong, flowing curves that not only provide a real feeling of space and movement, but lead the eye away from what are, almost inevitably, rectangular boundaries.

In other words, close to the house you should be thinking of using simple, rectangular shapes – crisp pre-cast slabs, brick paving or blocks, and raised beds – all of which can interlock and overlap to build up an interesting pattern. This approach would exclude materials such as crazy paving, as the conflicting lines and inherently 'busy' pattern clash with the house. If you want to use crazy paving (and remember, it is difficult to lay well) think of a more informal area, perhaps at the bottom of the garden, where it could provide an attractive sitting area, softened and surrounded by planting.

Formal or informal?

These are terms often bandied about by designers and gardening writers and many people think that they are the only styles available. This, of course, is not the case; and, moreover, the differ-

An unusual, modern symmetrical design.

ence is rather less than clear cut. A formal or symmetrical design is one that is 'mirrored' about a central axis, from one side or end of the composition to the other. Such designs are largely 'set pieces' and tend to appear to be static in their overall layout. They are often seen, and are of course suitable, around period houses or in municipal parks. On a smaller scale, a formal layout can be well employed for a herb or rose garden, where these features are part of an altogether different overall garden design.

An asymmetrical design is quite the opposite of a formal layout; you are seeking to create balance rather than a perfectly symmetrical image. Most people, when they think of dividing up a line pleasingly, will instinctively make that division towards one end of the line, rather than right in the middle. This aesthetic preference for asymmetry is the basis of the principles of composition in painting or drawing — and it applies to the art of garden design too. It is the same idea as trying to balance two unequal weights around a fulcrum: to bring both into equilibrium, the heavier weight will have to be nearer the fulcrum.

Much contemporary design uses this principle and in gardens it can be particularly effective. In practical terms, it means that, for example, the obvious bulk of a patio adjoining sliding doors on one side of the house might be countered by a smaller sitting area, seat and pool, further down the garden on the opposite side. Or a well planted border, sweeping out into the lawn, might find its equilibrium with a group of well chosen trees elsewhere.

You don't have to be a designer to 'feel' if something looks right, all you have to do is be honest and forget a lot of the preconceived ideas that have built up over a period of time.

Very often you can take basic ideas and 'pat-

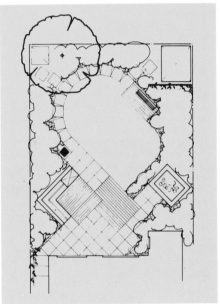

This diagonal plan makes the most of limited space.

terns' from somewhere quite unrelated to gardening — a wallpaper, fabric or carpet, for example; if the basic arrangement of shapes works in one design medium it is very often just as successful in another.

Don't necessarily think that a design has to go straight up and down a garden. Sometimes you can turn the whole pattern at an angle of, say, 45 degrees to the house. If you do this it is worth remembering that a diagonal line is the longest distance across a rectangle, and a garden planned in this way will maximise the space available and tend to look larger than it really is.

What shape is your garden?

Gardens come in all shapes and sizes, from square, through thin and wide, triangular, dog-legged, to many-sided. Of course you will still have to work out your requirements, whatever the shape, and these will have to be fitted within the confines of the boundaries. That said, there are different ways to handle different shapes.

Long and narrow
This is one of the most common and easily handled shapes of garden, especially in inter-war properties. Unfortunately, the standard way in which this shape is handled involves a path right down the middle, flanked by a border and washing line and finished with long straight beds around the perimeter. The end result is much like dressing a tall thin man in a pin-striped suit; it emphasises his height, or, in our case, the length of the garden.

Instead, think of breaking up the space into a series of rectangles, each one embracing a different purpose or theme. In this way you might have a patio of ample size close to the house, separated from the next 'room', of lawn, perhaps, by a wing of planting or a well positioned archway. Beyond this, you could position a small vegetable

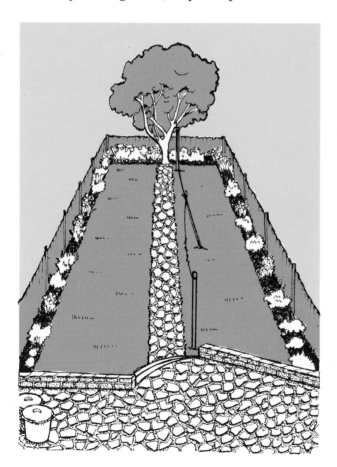

The layout of this long, narrow garden accentuates the awkward shape.

The author's garden: different 'rooms' for sitting, play and so on are created within the long shape.

garden, play area or group of fruit trees, while the furthest space of all could be given over to utility, shed and greenhouse. On page 21 you can see a photograph of my own garden which illustrates all these points. It also shows that, because the plot is on a gentle slope, broad steps are used to link the various areas together. You will also see that the path moves from side to side of the garden, and this also helps to open the space up, increasing the width visually.

Square

Where a long rectangular garden has a positive feeling of movement in a particular direction, a

If you have a lovely view beyond your garden, a minimal boundary can 'borrow' it for you.

square garden is completely static. In consequence it is the most difficult shape to handle.

If you are lucky enough to have a good view, you can turn your composition towards that and 'borrow' the space outside the plot to good advantage. More often than not, however, we are faced with four walls or fences that simply compound the problem.

In this case, there are a number of solutions. The first approach is to detract from the boundaries by creating a garden that 'turns in upon itself': that is, it has a central focal point and is designed so that the eye naturally moves towards it.

Here, a circular pattern can positively lead the eye away from the surroundings, focusing upon a

The static shape of this square garden is accentuated by the layout

Movement can be created within a static shape by a design that leads the eye in a spiral.

Interlocking rectangles of hard and soft surfaces, and planting, here create an interesting composition within a square garden.

centrally placed or off-set feature, which might be a statue or well positioned seat.

A second solution would echo rather than detract from the underlying square shape. Here one could eliminate curves altogether, using a series of interlocking rectangles that overlap one another to set up a pattern of their own. Each rectangle or series of rectangles could be made up from different surfaces and materials: different kinds of paving, built-in seating, water and planting. Such a pattern could also embrace changes of level, with steps providing a common denominator to link the composition together.

As another solution, remember that we have already seen the advantages of turning the design at an angle to the boundaries. This works particularly well in a square garden and provides the ideal opportunity to create a series of 'rooms', one overlapping or leading on from the next.

'Dog-legs'
There are many gardens that are not straightforward, and perhaps the most common of these is the one that disappears around a corner. All too often the two parts are treated as separate entities, each part of the garden having a different theme and purpose, with little to link them together.

In these circumstances, try to use a fluid pattern that leads both feet and eye through the space. A path and pergola may be useful here, as will well planned borders that reinforce the ground plan. Remember that mystery and surprise are two key elements in garden design and a garden of this shape is the ideal vehicle for both.

Using curves

Straight lines and rectangles may be all very well close to the house, but curves come into their own in the middle and distant parts of the garden. We have already seen the importance of using sensible geometric shapes, and this theme can be continued in the more informal parts of the design.

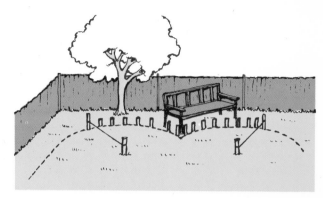

Use a line the length of the radius swung from a central cane to denote the curve.

Many books tell you the best way to shape a border is by throwing a hosepipe on the ground, arranging it in a haphazard line and taking an edging iron to cut out the resulting pattern: DON'T!

Curves, like any other part of the design, need to relate strongly not only to one another but also to the other parts of the design. The best and most sensible way to plan them is by using a pair of compasses, so that one curve flows into another. Play around with curves until you find a pleasing set of shapes that will give continuity to your design. Such shapes can easily be transferred on to the ground. Position a cane as the centre of the curve, scaling up the radius from the plan, and attach a line of the correct length to the cane. Swing this round and denote the path of the curve you want with sand or carefully positioned short stakes. Such strong shapes often seem severe on the plan, but when softened by several years of planting they look perfect.

Levels

In a small garden, too many changes of level can detract from, rather than enhance, the overall design. If there is a steep slope, retaining walls are

Pleasing curves in paths, lawns and borders create a soft but structured effect.

going to be essential and it will make sense to construct these in materials that blend with those used elsewhere in the design. If the change of level is not too severe, it can be more restful to slope a lawn or planted area, compensating a cross-fall on one side with taller plants or trees on the other.

Light and shade

In many parts of the world where the light is brighter than ours is, designers know the advantages of creating areas of sun and shadow. Such shadows create drama, highlighting a given area and offering the opportunity to sit in a cool place rather than in full sun. Although our temperate climate creates softer patterns, the light is quite strong enough to reinforce a design. A tree can cast a pool of shadow between two garden areas, and a pergola or arch sets up a tunnel of shade that draws one to a focal point or brightly lit view beyond.

The extendable garden

On page 28 you can see two designs, one very simple, the other rather more complicated. What they have in common is the fact that their basic layout is the same; however, any number of extra components can be added to the other simpler design at a later date, in order to extend and develop it. This approach could be ideal where an initial budget is limited, because it allows the garden to be built up and extended over a period of time.

To create a design like this, work out your ideal garden and separate all the components. The starting point can be as simple as you like and the length of time to completion is also entirely up to you.

Steep slopes need retaining walls, whereas gentle falls can just be clothed in grass or planting (above, top and bottom). A focal point can be important in a shady area (right).

26

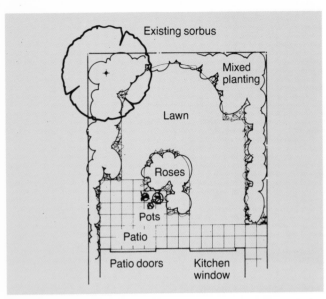

This basic 'extendable' layout has all the essential elements of a garden.

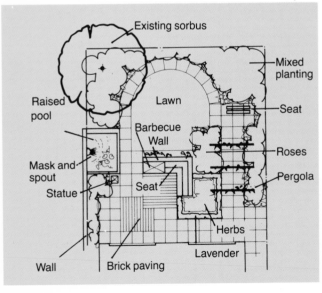

Once time and cash permit, other features can easily be added to the 'extendable' layout.

The rough design

It's finally time to begin working on your design! The check-list of features that you previously drew up (page 14) now really comes into its own, and it can be useful to rearrange this into an order of priority. In other words, a patio of ample size might be rather more important to you than an area for salad crops, and considerably more so than a statue, though of course you want to include all these things.

Once you have made your list, consider the most suitable location for each feature. It will be both useful and practical if your main sitting area is adjacent to sliding glass doors or French windows, but if this part of the garden is in shade for much of the day, a minimal amount of paving would be all that is required, with a linking path to a patio in the sun.

As far as access around the house and garden is concerned, just rough in where the new paths or hard-standing areas should go. These will then tend to tie in with other items from the check-list, such as a neatly combined dustbin and fuel store close to the back door, a paved play space in view of the kitchen window and perhaps a shelter to store the bikes and larger wheeled toys.

Now is the time to consider how a prevailing wind might spoil the pleasure of sitting somewhere particular, so some form of shelter could be roughly positioned. On the other hand where is the best place to catch that good view, or be screened from a bad one?

Vegetables, salad crops or herbs, should you wish to grow them, need not always be at the bottom of the garden; might it not be far more practical to put them closer to the house, in a more decorative form perhaps? The garden shed, small greenhouse, compost heap and incinerator should be thought about and paths again routed

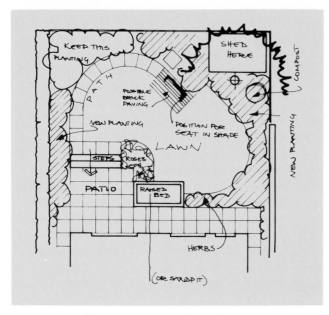

*When you are sure of your design,
make a neat copy of it for future use.*

in their direction. Play equipment, play space, a children's growing patch, and, of course, the washing line: all need to be given an initial rough location. Trees can give shelter, cast shade, provide visual 'punctuation' and emphasis, frame a good view or screen a bad one. Consider where to put them to best carry out these functions: they are a fundamental element of the architecture of the garden.

You can now see both the importance of the check-list and the sense of just roughing in just what goes where. It is amazing how many necessary features go into the average small garden, and it is very easy indeed to leave something out, if you have not been disciplined early on.

These days, there is often little division between front and back gardens, and so it can be useful – if the plan of the estate or street permits

– to site some of the items in your front garden. I have planned many patio areas in the front garden, particularly in older properties where space between house and road is ample and there is adequate screening from pedestrians and traffic. The position of the sun pays no respect to architecture, so while the back garden may be in shade all day, the front could be the opposite.

While on the subject of front gardens, noise can be a real problem in them, as it could be in the back if you have an adjoining playground! Much can be done with gently contoured banks and heavy planting to reduce noise, so again rough in where the problem occurs and where such a bank might be best sited. Pollution from traffic need not be a problem, because there are many tough, largely evergreen shrubs that will thrive in such conditions.

These initial 'rough' designs are just that: they can be easily changed, are fluid in their approach and, as stressed earlier, are ideal for trying out the ideas of the whole family. Never throw any of them away, for the simple reason that as they change and develop the design will start to 'firm up' and eventually reach a stage where it can be finalised.

The finished design

We have already seen that there is nothing difficult about formulating design ideas, and the finished plan is similarly straightforward. Remember that a good design is not only tailored to what you want but arranges those requirements in a simple, practical and above all uncomplicated way. Keep remembering that arranging the components in the garden is little different from organising furniture in a room: it is, if you like, pattern-making and if the pattern is unattractive then the garden will be too.

The design that you finally evolve is the ground plan of your new garden and can be drawn to scale on a sheet of tracing paper laid over squared or graph paper. Use the same scale that you used for the survey and accurately plot the position of paved areas, raised beds, seating, barbecue, lawns, buildings, trees and so on.

Make a model

Just occasionally, some people find it almost impossible to visualise a finished garden from a plan, even if they have put the information together over a period of time. If this is the case, a simple model can help enormously. Cut out the various components of the plan, stick them on card and raise or lower them to correspond with any changes of level. Form simple blocks to represent planted areas and make trees also from cut-outs. Colour them in and view the finished garden from all directions; it can be very helpful.

Equally, a view from an upstairs window, when the garden shapes have been carefully pegged out to scale, can give you a much better idea of the final look. In other words, don't be afraid to work out the design in the way that suits you best. It is crucial to appreciate all the implications of the design: after all, it has not only to look right, but also to work effectively as a framework for the family's outdoor activities.

The finished pattern

All the points mentioned in this chapter are aspects of the total scheme. You may not need or wish to incorporate all of them, but if you check them off, one by one, they will give you a sensible framework within which you can work.

We have already seen the value of a well-thought-out design in terms of suitability for you and your family, as the basis for obtaining competitive quotations and as a starting point for doing-it-yourself. Perhaps the most important advantage is that, with a clearly-thought-out initial concept, you can build the garden over a period of time without losing sight of that initial all-important vision.

PREPARING THE SITE

Anybody who has carried out work inside the home on a do-it-yourself basis knows the importance of sound preparation, whether for decoration or any other project. The principles are exactly the same in your outside room, and although much of this work will go unseen it will pay enormous dividends later on when you come to plant the garden or lay your finished surfaces.

Changes in level

A sloping garden can be a great asset in terms of design, but it can also pose all kinds of problems. A flat garden, on the other hand, can benefit from the introduction of gentle and generous contoured mounds. You might also want to use excavations from a swimming pool in this way, or to screen a bad view, or, in conjunction with planting, to help soak up the sound of a busy road.

Mounds and banks can be created either by bringing in top soil or by using material already on site. If thinking of the latter you will almost certainly use a 'cut and fill' technique, where soil is dug from one place and deposited in another. Whatever the method, make sure that the finished levels are always covered with an adequate depth of topsoil, the fertile layer that can support plant growth. An adequate depth for shrubs will be approximately 30 cm (12 inches) while grass will grow on about half that depth.

The shape in which you form a bank will be important too, gentle contours being far more restful in a small garden than sharply chiselled slopes. Such slopes will also be subject to less erosion than a steep bank, where rain can quickly wash away both new planting and the topsoil in which it grows.

The positioning of a bank is equally crucial to its success within the design. You can't just put it down anywhere! Think about it in relation to the shapes and relationships of the other parts of the plan.

If you have difficulty visualising the finished bank, peg the shape out with a series of canes

Changes in level: here broad, generous steps link a patio with a sunken lawn pleasingly.

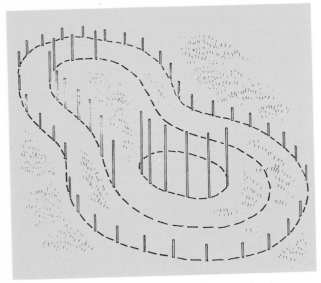

*To visualise a bank, use canes of different heights
to mark out its contours.*

have the effect of creating flat, or slightly sloping, platforms, each of which will not only be more manageable than the original slope but can be given a different theme or purpose, for example: children's play area; orchard; rock outcrops; different colour themes and so on. The same visual rules apply here as in other parts of the garden, and you should build the walls from similar materials to those used elsewhere. The shape and line of such walls close to the house and surrounding or supporting a patio will look more comfortable laid out to an architectural design; those further away may be curved to reflect the underlying theme. Areas towards the top of the garden may well be allowed to retain their natural slope and this too will help to create a feeling of distance and space.

While retaining walls may be necessary, remember that access will be important too, not just for people but possibly for a mower and other

and indicate the height at various points in the same way. By doing this you can get a good idea of the likely amount of screening, as well as being able to estimate the volume of soil required.

If your garden slopes up from the house it will tend to foreshorten the view, and appear to make the space feel smaller than it really is; if it drops away the opposite will be the case. These are factors that you need to bear in mind when preparing the design. If the slopes are gentle there is little problem, but if the level changes are considerable, and on many new housing estates they certainly are, then a rather more far-reaching approach is needed.

Retaining walls
This approach may well be a combination of the 'cut and fill' technique just mentioned, with the construction of retaining walls to hold the levels thus formed in place (see pages 46-7). This will

*Changes in level: the junction between patio
and retaining wall has been cleverly softened by planting.*

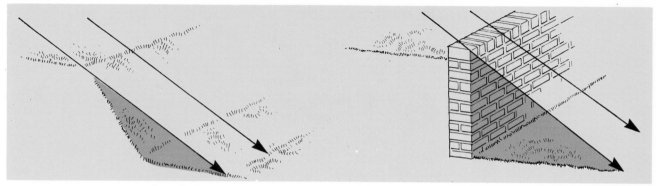

Less shade is cast by a gentle slope (left) than by a retaining wall (right).

machinery. It may well be that you decide to buy a lightweight portable machine, but if you don't, ramps as well as steps may well be needed.

Such steps and ramps will form a 'tension point' in the design, which will draw the eye and create a feeling of expectancy that increases as you get closer and is released as you pass into the next 'room'. Position them carefully. Remember that any slope may be difficult for the elderly or disabled, and so a gently sloping ramp may be ideal for them too. The creation of shade will be another factor to bear in mind; a slope may have a reasonably open aspect, but a retaining wall may cast deep shadows along its length.

Another direct consequence of adjusting levels will be the effect this has on the water-table (the natural height of water in the ground). If you lower the garden at any point, the water-table will be nearer the surface. Any planting, and particularly trees, is susceptible to variations of this kind: a mature tree can be killed by a change in level of as little as 15 cm (6 inches). When using 'cut and fill' to terrace a garden, any retaining wall should be at least 1 metre (3 feet) away from the trunk, and particular care should be taken not to sever any roots, thus making the tree unstable.

Drainage

For a soil to be able to support healthy plant growth and essential organisms it needs two things: air and water. Waterlogged soils lack air, which is essential for extraction of nutrients from soil by roots. If plants are shallow-rooted because of inadequate drainage, they are not only poorly anchored but are unable to obtain sufficient nutrients.

The causes of poor drainage are several: it could be due to a sticky clay soil, a hard 'pan' of soil (usually caused by compaction) some way below the surface that is preventing moisture from percolating away, or a high water-table.

Contrary to common belief, clay soils are normally fertile and rich in nutrients, their sticky nature helping to retain the necessary chemicals that benefit plant growth. On the debit side, they are difficult to work, slow to warm up and also present drainage problems. The introduction of organic matter, such as compost, manure or peat, helps to open the soil up and allow freer percolation of water.

Where a 'pan' lies some way beneath the surface, it is necessary to break it up physically by deep digging. This type of problem is often found on new housing estates, where site traffic has compacted the soil and then a fresh layer of topsoil has been imported and laid on top. When purchasing a new property, try to ensure that the builder breaks the ground for you before you move in.

The height of a water-table will vary throughout the year, but under ideal conditions it will lie about 1.8 m (6 feet) below the ground. Where there are permanently boggy conditions and these are not due to a 'pan' or an unusually heavy soil, the water-table will be almost at ground level. In this case, artificial drainage will be necessary if you are going to be successful in growing plants.

Laying drains
Land drains can be constructed either from earthenware pipes laid end to end, or from perforated plastic pipes. The latter come in long sections

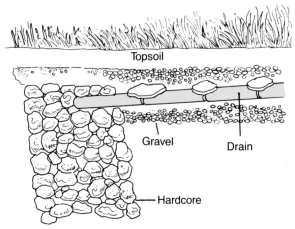

A drain and soakaway.

that can be bent around corners; they should be laid in trenches that are 60–90 cm (2–3 feet) deep on a 10 cm (4-inch) layer of gravel. Cover the drain with gravel before finally replacing the top-

Changes in level: an interesting combination of materials has been used in this sloping garden.

Changes in level: in this garden under construction, a raised bed has been positioned to 'punctuate' the long and narrow shape.

soil. The fall, or slope, of the drain should be approximately 1 in 200, and it can be directed either into a soakaway or into a ditch. Do not run surface water drains into the house drainage system; it contravenes building regulations. Also remember that your neighbour will be justifiably upset if you pipe water into his plot!

Improving the soil

The better you can make your soil, the more it will repay you in terms of produce, flower and foliage. You can do this by adding organic or inorganic fertilisers and conditioners; the former kind has definite advantages.

Organic fertilisers

The addition of organic matter, in the form of manure or well rotted compost, helps to form humus, which in turn is essential to support plant growth. Humus is a brown, crumbly substance made from decaying organic matter. Soil bacteria need humus to survive, and soil needs the bacteria to stay healthy. Adding humus will also 'condition' or improve the soil structure, lightening a sticky clay and helping to bind together a sandy soil.

Perhaps one of the most valuable pieces of equipment in the garden is a good compost bin or heap. Locate it sensibly in a screened position with good wheelbarrow access. To get the best from it, ensure it is in the shade. Many materials are compostable, including organic kitchen waste, lawn-mowings (but not if you have used a hormone weed-killer), annual weeds (not perennial ones, which are likely to start growing again), flowerheads, softwood prunings and leaves of all kinds. Keep clear of any material that is diseased, or you could spread the disease in the compost.

Peat will also improve the soil texture, but should not be treated as a fertiliser. Because it is dark it absorbs heat, and the soil will tend to warm up more quickly as a result.

Other organic conditioners include sawdust, wood chips and seaweed, which is also a good source of nutrients and is in ready supply near the coast. Spent mushroom compost and spent hops offer rather less nutrition but have good conditioning properties. 'Blood, fish and bone' is an excellent all-round organic fertiliser.

Inorganic fertilisers

Inorganic fertilisers and conditioners can improve soil texture and fertility, but do not on their own support the soil bacteria vital for keeping the ground in good heart. They should therefore be used carefully, together with organic material if at all possible.

Conditioners include materials such as sharp sand, grit and ash. All of these will be particularly helpful in opening up a heavy soil.

Fertilisers in this category are faster acting than organics, and contain the elements nitrogen (N), phosphorus (P) and potassium (K). This should be stated clearly on the pack or bottle, but do check, because some fertilisers only contain one of these. A good example of an excellent all-round fertiliser is Growmore.

Cultivation

One might wonder, since plants grow naturally on uncultivated ground, why we should need to prepare our gardens so thoroughly. The reasons for this have already been outlined: preparing and conditioning the soil means that young plants can grow easily, minimising weed growth; and it allows us to dig in composts and fertilisers.

The best time to dig is in the autumn, so that frost and rain can break down the roughly turned ground. Don't dig in frosty conditions or when the ground is waterlogged. This can not only be back-breaking work, but can do more harm than good by compacting the soil too much.

The methods by which ground can be prepared vary in their degrees of thoroughness; most common is single digging, for which you will need a good garden spade and fork.

The technique involves digging the plot over in strips. Start by turning over the first trench, to one spade's depth, and removing the soil to the point where you are going to finish digging. If you wish to incorporate manure, fork it lightly into the bottom of the trench and turn the next strip of ground over on top of it. Always make sure you remove all perennial weeds: docks, bindweed and

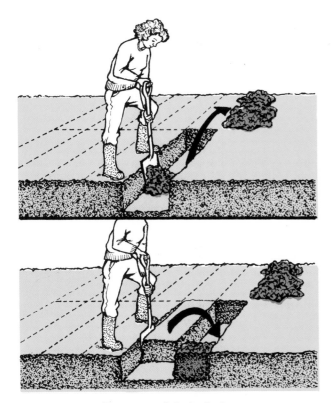

*The stages of single digging:
this should be done every autumn.*

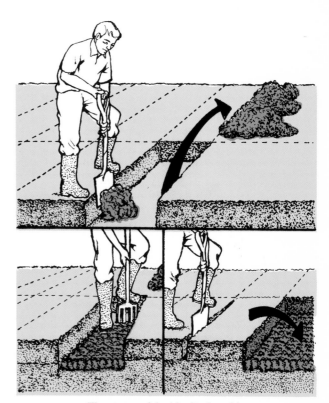

*The stages of double digging: this
need only be carried out every few years.*

ground elder are the worst. Take out every particle of root, otherwise the plants will quickly regenerate and you will have to carry out the whole task again.

This technique of digging in strips and throwing the soil forwards into the trench just formed can be continued right across the area involved. The last job will be to fill the final trench with the soil that you took from the very first strip.

The secret when digging or cultivating any piece of ground is to take it in easy stages; there is never any point in becoming the slave of your garden and if a job becomes tedious you not only

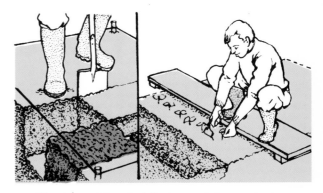

*The stages of deep-bed digging: work from a plank
to avoid compressing the soil.*

run the risk of physical exhaustion – or worse – but you also become fed up and in consequence fail to do the job properly.

Double digging *is* hard work and only really needs to be carried out when there is a hard sub-soil pan that is preventing proper drainage, or if the ground has never been dug before.

The process is similar to single digging in that you remove a spade's depth of soil from the first trench and position it ready to fill the last. However, once the bottom of that first trench is exposed it is forked over to a further full spade's depth and plenty of organic material is dug in. The second trench is turned into the one just dug and so the process continues.

Both of the above methods are suitable for ornamental borders and vegetables. A method that is becoming increasingly popular for the latter is the 'deep bed system'. This involves double digging in the usual way introducing plenty of compost and manure. To avoid compacting the soil, and this is very important, the vegetable garden is divided up into relatively narrow beds, just over a metre wide. These can be worked either from paths or from platforms laid across the beds. If you use this system you should only have to dig the ground thoroughly again after five or six years: a real saving in time and energy. When crops are lifted, simply hoe the ground over and lightly fork manure or compost into the surface of the beds.

Good tools are vital to correct cultivation. Keep them sharp, clean them after use and lightly oil them before putting them away. If you really want to indulge yourself use stainless steel, which slips through the ground like butter. A full description of tools can be found on pages 135–8.

If, on the other hand, you have physical difficulty in digging, you may think of buying one of the excellent spring-loaded spades that are on the market. They really do make the job a great deal easier and in my opinion can do it just as well.

BOUNDARIES

From what we have learned so far, it is obvious that successful gardens are complex creations! A garden is made from a number of interlocking components and of these, the materials used to define the boundaries are crucial to the way the garden hangs together.

By now you will probably have a pretty good idea of the type of fence or wall that you can sensibly afford and which will harmonise with the surrounding locality and general environment.

Of course in certain situations – an open-plan area or a garden set within a rural landscape – there may be no reason for a boundary at all, and here you could turn your attention to providing internal walls and screens. These will help to provide that feeling of space division and surprise that we discussed earlier, both of which should be integral parts of a well designed outdoor room. Hedges may well achieve much the same result and these we discuss in greater detail a little later in this chapter. Hedges also form an ideal habitat for a wide range of wildlife.

A boundary can do rather more than just provide a physical barrier to unwelcome people and animals. As well as preventing access it also keeps your children and pets secure inside. If of a sufficient height it can break a sight-line and afford welcome privacy; it will also dampen down noise and block off a bad view, if one exists. It will provide shelter, and can act as a frame to emphasise or enhance a particularly good aspect.

Choosing the right type of boundary

You have only to visit a large garden centre or walk down a suburban street to see the vast range of wall materials available — but the insensitive way in which they are often used is also fairly obvious!

It is worth underlining the importance of choosing a boundary material that is compatible with the style of your house. Local building techniques (if there are any) should influence what you choose. A stone wall adjoining a stone cottage looks just right, and that is why people flock to such places as the Cotswolds, where they can see materials used in a sympathetic way. A continuing tradition of using local materials harmoniously, linked to sensible planning controls, does much to ensure that our countryside, country towns and villages remain reasonably visually intact. When you go on holiday abroad it is easy to see how quickly a superb landscape is destroyed by insensitive development.

Cost will, of course, be a second important factor in your choice; the 'hard landscape' elements of fencing, walling and paving are likely to account for up to 75 per cent of your total garden budget. This being the case, and bearing in mind that walls are expensive, you may sensibly think of fencing as your main boundary material. There will be a wide choice, but again it will make sense to try and relate fencing to an overall architectural style. Traditional woven fences, such as wattle hurdles and osiers, are still used in certain parts of the country; these may often look superb in a more suburban setting, if there is no overriding contradictory style, particularly in association with well planted borders.

Lately there has been a fad for using 'ranch fencing', which can look fine adjoining crisp contemporary buildings and painted to continue a particular colour scheme. Adjoining a Victorian villa, it can look very contrived and a simple interwoven panel or close board fence will be far more workmanlike, blending sensibly into the background. This is just what any boundary should do: it should not set out to be a feature in its own right.

One can outline the advantages and disadvantages of various boundaries as follows.

Fences
Advantages   Cheaper than walls; easier to erect; certain types (such as chain-link, netting or slatted) retain a view while at the same time offering security.

Disadvantages   Higher maintenance; access needed for maintenance (i.e. a service strip or path); less effective in reducing noise; not so strong.

Walls
Advantages   Stronger; better at reducing noise; offer complete privacy if high enough; provide shelter; minimal maintenance.

Disadvantages   Expensive; difficult for the amateur to build; difficult to move.

Hedges
Advantages   Cheap; excellent wind break when established; good screening if evergreen; blend well into most gardens.

Disadvantages   Slow to establish; need regular clipping (some types more than others); lack of privacy in the short term; may be poisonous.

The list should allow you to make a reasoned choice of the type of boundary you may wish to use; we can now survey what is available in greater detail.

Natural stone walls

Provided that the locality in which it is used is taken into account, stone is one of the finest boundary materials available. It is durable, it mellows beautifully with age and it brings great visual stability to a setting. It can be obtained either 'dressed', in finished blocks of various sizes, or 'random'. The former is largely the province of the craftsman stonemason; the latter is far more adaptable for home use.

Dry stone walls can be laid in either random or regular courses, and should be built with a slight angle or 'batter' to either face. This means that the wall is slightly wider at the bottom than at the top. Traditionally, the foundations were minimal, usually a wide course of stones just below ground level. If building in a domestic garden, however, one should think of using a concrete foundation of 6:1. That is, six parts of aggregate (a mixture of sand and small stones bought from builders' merchants) to one part cement. Make it approximately one-and-a-half times as wide as the base of the wall. The depth should be about 30 cm (1 foot), depending on the type of soil.

Whether regularly or randomly coursed, the wall should incorporate 'through stones' at regular heights and intervals; these help to tie the wall together and provide added stability. The centre of the wall is usually filled with smaller stones, rubble and chippings left over from fashioning the various pieces, while the coping (the top of the wall) can be constructed from stones laid on edge, side by side.

Dry stone walls are beautiful in themselves and set off planting superbly.

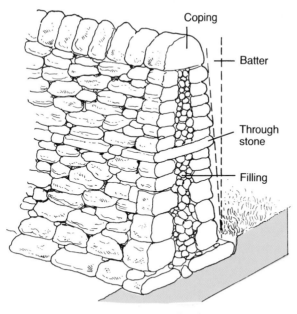

*Constructing a dry stone wall – shown
in cross-section.*

Such a wall takes time, patience and a degree of skill to build, but if they can stick with it – and there is no doubt it is an enormously satisfying job – most people can make a very fair attempt.

The suburban version uses mortar; while this can look reasonable if well carried out, the result more often than not ends up looking like a dry stone wall with joints oozing toothpaste! This technique should be avoided like the plague by the amateur. A dry stone wall has additional advantages: pockets and crevices along its face are ideal for the introduction of creeping and Alpine plants. The habit architects and surveyors have of advising their clients to rip vegetation from any wall on the basis that it does damage is largely unnecessary, unless there is already severe structural decay. Natural stone also has a delightful tendency to grow mosses and lichens and this can be encouraged on a new wall by the application of yogurt or liquid manure.

Brick walls

Brick is a widely used and attractive material for building walls. Its small size makes it suitable for a domestic situation and the wide range of colours and textures in which it is available usually ensures a close match with that used in the house. Because a free-standing wall has both faces open to the weather, make sure that you use a durable brick; a few of the very old types of 'stock' bricks tend to be too soft for walling.

Traditionally, free-standing brick walls were built two bricks or 21.5 cm (9 inches) thick, finished with a sensible coping of 'brick on edge' (bricks laid side by side). Alternative copings, which keep the weather out of the top of the wall, could include a neat pre-cast strip,

*If mortar is used in a stone wall, it must be
carefully pointed.*

Brick ages beautifully, and sets off plants well.

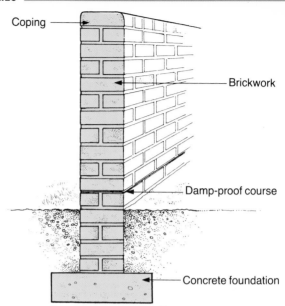

Coping
Brickwork
Damp-proof course
Concrete foundation

Constructing a brick wall – in cross-section.

paving slabs, tiles to match the house, or, in some instances, a zinc or copper strip.

Today you see all kinds of walls which are only a single brick thick and consequently buttressed at regular intervals. While this approach can be a reasonable one, the coping often presents a problem, and the habit of standing bricks on end (or even worse, at an angle) lacks visual stability and should be avoided.

A curved or 'serpentine' wall is stronger than a straight run. Another solution to the problem of strength, particularly in a front garden, might be to stagger the pattern so that right-angled sections of wall interlock with one another to form an interesting composition, with planting filling the gaps to soften the outline. This approach, or a serpentine wall, will also create shadow patterns, which could be another factor in the overall design.

Foundations should be twice as wide as the wall, constructed from concrete (6 : 1) and approximately 45 cm (18 inches) deep for a 1.8 m (6-foot) wall. The depth can vary depending on the soil conditions: over solid rock you need far less; on wet ground rather more.

Damp-proof course
A damp-proof course prevents moisture from moving up the wall from the ground and therefore prolongs the life of the brickwork. Traditionally a damp proof course was of two or three courses of a hard 'engineering' brick, slate or even lead. Engineering brick was often used because of its contrasting colour; it still can be used as a decorative element, although a bituminous strip is rather more often employed today.

Expansion joints
Because of differences in temperature, and ground movements and vibrations from traffic, a wall will tend to move slightly along its length. If the wall is built in a continuous run, there will be a tendency for cracks to appear: you can quite often see this. If the wall is less than about 10 m

(33 feet) long, there should be little problem; if it is longer it is sensible to build it in sections of approximately 9 m (30 feet) leaving a gap of 10 mm (⅜ inch) between each run.

Bonds

The pattern in which the wall is built creates brick bonds, which give the whole structure strength. Some are stronger than others, for example, Flemish bond. For domestic purposes all the recognised bonds are more than sufficient.

Pointing

Bricks are laid with mortar joints. The correct strength of mortar is four parts sand to one part cement, plus plasticiser. Plasticiser helps keep the mixture workable, but too much can make the mortar weak. Buy it from the builders' merchants and add according to packet directions.

The way the joints are finished or 'pointed' on

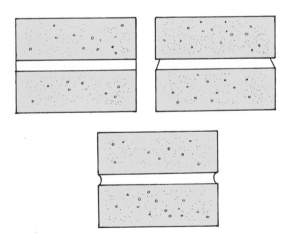

The simplest and most common styles for pointing: 'flush', 'weathered' and 'keyed'.

the face of the wall can make a great deal of difference to the end result. Joints can be flush, weathered, keyed, raked out or rubbed back. The deeper the joint (maximum 6 mm, to retain weather resistance), the more clearly each brick stands out in relief. Old bricks that were often hand-made and irregular usually look best if slightly raked.

As a guide to estimating quantities you will need 120 bricks per square (face) metre of double thickness or 21.5 cm (9-inch) wall and half that amount for an 11 cm (4½-inch wall).

Concrete

Concrete is a much-maligned material for both paving and walling; this is a great pity, as it can produce a handsome, durable finish that is very cost-effective and usually far quicker to build than either brick or stone.

Blocks usually measure about 45 x 22.5 x 22.5 cm (18 x 9 x 9 inches), and in many modern housing schemes they form the ideal boundary between two properties. Some blocks have an almost smooth face, and these can easily be colour-washed to link with a paint scheme inside the house, thus providing an ideal link between house and garden. If the surface is less smooth, the face of the wall can be cement-rendered; if you do this avoid the temptation to make patterns in the surface, which simply look contrived! The most suitable coping for a wall of this type is brick laid on edge.

On the debit side, concrete blocks are heavy and this makes such a wall hard work to build. Once you get above a comfortable working height, erect firm staging that will eliminate lifting the blocks awkwardly into position. Like most jobs in the garden, take things in easy stages and

Concrete can be a surprisingly attractive walling material if sensitively used.

there will be few problems.

Concrete screen blocks are always popular and come in a wide range of patterns, which by their very nature tend to look 'busy'. They offer little in the way of privacy or shelter and to look reasonable need to be clothed in bold-leafed climbing plants. Because they are 'stack-bonded', that is, one exactly on top of another without overlapping joints, the walls have no great strength and need to be built with purpose-made pilasters or piers at regular intervals. The overall effect doesn't really blend into the background restfully, and frankly looks suburban in the extreme.

A well-thought-out fence will almost certainly do the job as well and look a good deal better into the bargain.

Reconstituted stone

There are an increasing number of 'reconstituted' stone blocks coming on to the market. These are made from a mixture of cement and crushed stone. The colour of the material will vary depending on where the stone was quarried: Cotswold derivatives will be that familiar soft, yellow tone, while 'York' will be largely grey. Some

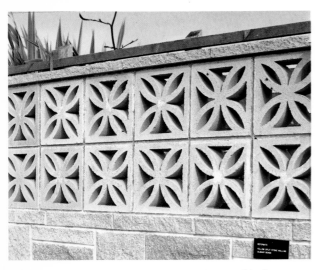

A wall of reconstituted stone, and screen blocks.

colour stone laid with a grey cement mortar: there are a whole range of mortar additives available that can be mixed in to match whatever material you are using.

Retaining walls

We talked about retaining walls in the previous chapter; if your garden is on a reasonable slope then you will almost certainly need to construct one or several walls of this type.

The same aesthetic rules apply as for any other wall; the real construction difference lies in the ability a retaining wall must have to withstand the action of soil and water pressure. If a wall needs to be more than about 1.2 m (4 feet) high, and you are not a skilled bricklayer familiar with the problems involved, it will be well worth your while to

of these blocks are excellent, particularly those that are specifically produced to look like crisp, rectangular, sawn pieces. These can look superb in the right setting, for example they might link with a similar natural stone in a period house. Rather more common and rather less effective are those blocks that try to simulate a rough-hewn stone. They are normally similar in size to bricks, and, to be fair, some are quite acceptable, provided that you use them in an honest fashion for what they are. Many new houses – particularly in traditional stone areas – are built with such blocks, and so garden walling using the same is sensible. The worst offenders are the larger blocks that are subdivided to look like several smaller stones. When these are built to form a wall they look just what they are, a very poor imitation.

The rule, then, is to pick your product carefully, avoiding the worse imitations. You should also pay attention to the colour of the mortar used for laying. There is nothing worse than a Cotswold-

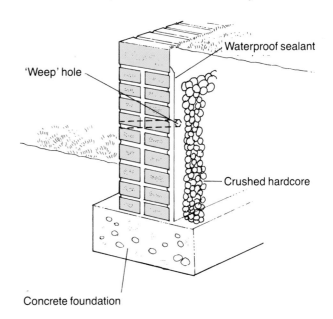

Constructing a brick retaining wall – in cross-section

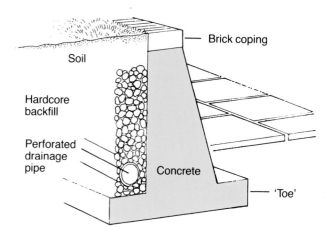

*Constructing a concrete retaining wall –
in cross-section.*

Brick coping

Soil

Hardcore
backfill

Perforated
drainage
pipe

Concrete

'Toe'

put the job out to a qualified landscaper or builder, who may in turn suggest the services of a qualified surveyor. The damage caused by a high retaining wall that fails can be both horrifying and expensive, so take sound advice.

If a wall is in the region of 1 m (3 feet) high and brickwork is used, it is advisable to build the bottom six or so courses 45 cm (18 inches) thick, as the greatest pressure will be against the lower section of the wall.

Concrete can be an excellent choice and this can be cast so that the bottom is wider than the top. It can also be built with a 'toe' that will react to pressure from the back and dig into the ground, providing extra stability. A cast-concrete or concrete-block wall can be faced with another material such as stone or brick, allowing it to match similar materials used elsewhere.

Water behind the wall increases the pressure on it. This can be relieved by putting drainage or 'weep' holes along the face every metre. Pipes should be built in 7.5 cm (3 inches) above the lower finished ground level, or joints in the brick-

work can be left open. To aid drainage, place a vertical layer of crushed hardcore or broken stone behind the wall, and to prevent deterioration of the brick or concrete, paint the back of the wall with a sealant.

In extreme conditions, lengths of reinforcing rod the same height as the wall can be cast into the foundation and concrete blocks built around these to provide additional stability.

Fences

The aesthetic rules that governed the choice of walling are just as applicable to fences. In other words, the use of plastic posts and chains to simulate timber and iron is visually dishonest. So too is a plastic ranch fence that imitates wood. It is

*Boulders can be used to define part of a boundary
and stop people walking over the plants.*

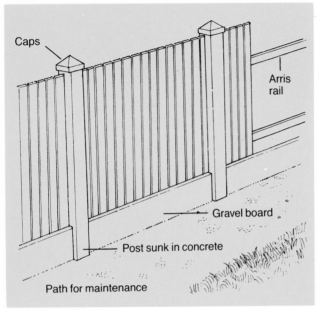

The basic style of fence construction.

Caps

Arris rail

Gravel board

Post sunk in concrete

Path for maintenance

made from the stems of that plant.

While these types of fence are usually individually made to order, most fences are mass-produced and sold as panels through your local garden centre.

Whatever the type of fence, its life will be greatly extended if it is regularly treated with preservative and constructed properly. Remember, therefore, that it may be sensible to plan a path next to a fence in order to carry out maintenance. Panels and posts should be capped to prevent penetration by moisture and the use of a replaceable 'gravel board' at the bottom of the run will minimise rot setting into the panels above.

If you can spend a little more and use hardwood posts, such as oak, they will last a good deal longer. Be sure never to use creosote as a preservative anywhere in the vicinity of plants, it means certain death for them. Use one of the excellent non-toxic preservatives that are formulated especially for garden use.

If you keep the posts at the same height as the panels, your fence will look less fussy than if they protrude by several inches. Remember that the posts are normally positioned on the side of the legal owner of the fence.

As posts bear the whole weight of the fence and as wind pressure can be enormous on a run, ensure that posts are securely fixed. They can be embedded in concrete, using six parts aggregate to one part cement; or use one of the square-section, pointed, steel sleeves that can be driven into the ground. These are specifically made so that a timber post can be fitted into them. Some types can be adjusted to bring them into an exactly vertical position.

While most of the styles of fence are set out below, remember that there is a great difference between open and solid or closed types. Of the

not that there is anything inherently wrong with using plastic: it has excellent advantages of durability and ease of care. The problem lies in using one material to look like another, when it should be honestly employed for what it is.

There are still a number of styles and patterns of fencing that have strong regional character. Of these, wattle hurdles are particularly attractive, being made from woven hazel stems in a range of heights and sizes. Originally used for penning sheep, they have made a natural transition into the garden; they blend well into most situations and look particularly good as a background to planting. Their life-expectancy is about ten years and they would make an ideal screen while a hedge or background of shrubs becomes established. Slightly different in look but having the same broad characteristics are osier panels, made from willow stems, and bamboo screens, former, a style such as 'post and rail' is ideal in a rural location, where the view is allowed in while the stock is kept out, the ideal link between garden and landscape. In town a 'ranch' style fence will do much the same thing, offering little in the way of privacy but perhaps linking with a particular architectural setting. The role of the fence in both these situations is to define a boundary rather than to provide screening or shelter.

Types of closed fence

There are two basic types of fence: open and closed. We will look at the varieties of each in detail, starting with closed, or solid, fences.

Panel fences

This is the most popular type of fence, which comes in a range of heights and sizes up to approximately 1.8×1.8 m (6×6 feet). Panels are set between timber or concrete posts; in the latter case the posts are recessed so that panels can neatly slot into place. If possible, use a gravel board at the bottom of the run (see above) and always avoid piling soil against a fence, as this will accelerate decay.

Any new fence, particularly in a virgin garden, looks austere and will almost certainly look better if softened by planting; climbers are particularly useful. In this case, train them on horizontal wires every 45 cm (18 inches), fixed with galvanised nails or vine eyes and stretched between the posts. This will minimise rot of the relatively thin fence slats and will make maintenance easier, because the wires can be taken down complete with the climber and refixed after work has been carried out.

Close board fences

This is a relatively expensive but durable type of fence and involves fixing overlapping vertical boards on to horizontal 'arris rails' that are in turn slotted into square posts set approximately 1.8 m (6 feet) apart. The advantage of this type of fence is that individual boards rather than whole panels can be replaced. When erecting a close board fence, therefore, keep a few extra boards in store for just such an eventuality.

Slatted fences

This type of fence is similar to close board, in that the vertical slats are fixed to arris rails and posts. The width of the slats ranges from 15 cm (6 inches) or more, down to approximately 5 cm (2 inches). If you leave a slight gap of say 15 mm (½ inch), this helps to produce a visually 'light' run that is most attractive. If you want a cheap solution, why not use old floorboards in this way? Clean them up and make sure that they are well treated with preservative. To produce an unusual design that could perhaps link with a particular garden or architectural style, you could vary the height of the slats to produce a staggered pattern.

Ranch fencing

Ranch fencing normally uses quite wide boards, fixed horizontally between posts. It has a strong architectural line and can look excellent in a contemporary setting running directly out from a building, perhaps being painted in the same colour as woodwork elsewhere on the house. If the boards are set on either side of the posts, they can completely break a sight line, and of course the fence can be as tall or short as necessary.

Wattle hurdles and osier fences

I have already mentioned these, and it is sufficient to say that they make a solid if relatively short-term fence. They look excellent in association with planting and are normally fixed with galvanised wire on to round, pointed stakes driven into the ground.

Types of open fence

There is also a variety of open-type fences.

Post and rail fences
This type can be either two- or three-rail and is a rural fence ideally suited to keeping stock out of a garden. It does not provide privacy or shelter but allows a good view to be seen. Painted white it is called a 'paddock' fence and looks pretentious in any setting except a genuine stud farm or race-course. Gates, unless five-bar, look out of place; the best method of crossing is by a well built stile.

Single rail fences
These are often used in front gardens to mark the boundaries between properties or with the pavement. Being only about 30 cm (1 foot) high, they provide no privacy, but they do direct both feet and eye towards a path or access point.

Picket fences
This is the type of fence that often frames the country cottage seen on so many chocolate boxes. In fact it looks fine in such a situation, but rather worse outside a suburban semi or 'stock-broker's Tudor' mansion. The height is usually about 90 cm (3 feet) and the tops can be either pointed or rounded. White or a simple stain are the preferred colours, the former needing rather more maintenance. A modern version is shown opposite; this looks neat in the right setting.

Post and chain fences
Traditionally, these were the counterpart of a single-rail fence, marking the edge of a property in an urban situation. They utilise cast-iron chains, painted black, with white posts. The imitation

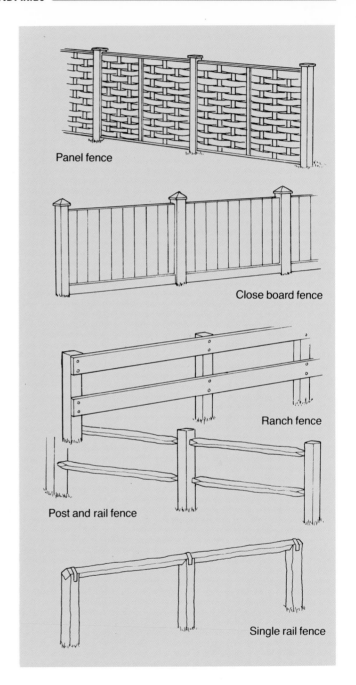

Panel fence

Close board fence

Ranch fence

Post and rail fence

Single rail fence

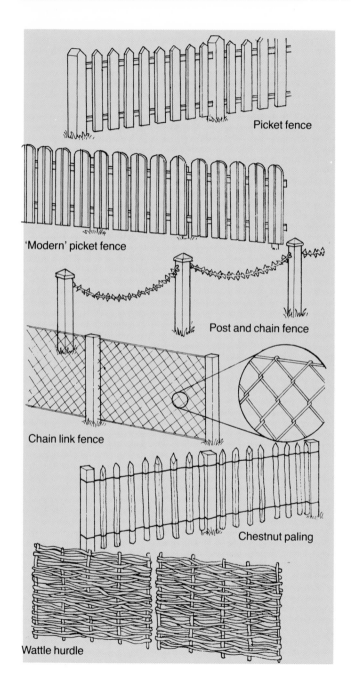

Picket fence

'Modern' picket fence

Post and chain fence

Chain link fence

Chestnut paling

Wattle hurdle

variety in plastic is awful, as is their use in anything but the setting of a fine period house.

Chain link fences

This is a durable style of fence and a good choice for security. It again comes in a variety of heights and should be firmly attached to stout metal posts. The plastic-coated variety lasts longer and posts can also be obtained treated in a similar way. Green is commonly available, but in fact both black and brown blend better into a garden or landscape setting. Sited within a heavy planting of shrubs it can be almost invisible, but in an open position looks institutional, needing the softening influence of climbing plants. It offers little in the way of privacy or shelter. The posts should be securely bedded in concrete.

Chestnut palings

These are normally about 1.2 m (4 feet) high and are best employed as a temporary fence or garden divider. The vertical pales are of cleft chestnut; they are joined together with galvanised wire and secured on to round, pointed posts driven into the ground. They can be very useful for keeping dogs and children off a particular area while it is becoming established, and can be bought or stored in rolls. As the palings are about 10 cm (4 inches) apart, they offer no privacy.

Gates

After putting a good deal of thought into the way to surround your property, it would be a great pity to spoil the end result with a poorly detailed or incorrect gate. The style of the latter does not necessarily have to match the boundary; in fact a contrast will help to highlight the point of entry and departure. However, as I have emphasised elsewhere, any focal point should be well

A gate should blend with its boundary in style and scale.

This mature hedge makes an unobtrusive background for a charming mixed border.

detailed, and the incongruity of a spindly, modern, wrought-iron gate set in a fine old traditional wall should by now be more than obvious.

The same criteria apply as for fences; there is little point in having a solid fence for privacy if the gate is of an open pattern. As a general rule, a gate should respect the height of the boundary involved, be simply and solidly built and be adequately fixed on a secure post or pier.

In a front garden you might think of combining the vehicle and pedestrian entrances so that the gate is divided into two unequal sections which can each be opened separately. This might well eliminate the common practice of having a separate path to the front door, which does much to overcomplicate what is usually a relatively small space.

Screens

We have already seen that by dividing a garden up into different areas we not only create different 'rooms' but add to a feeling of mystery or surprise, hence the usefulness of screens in a garden design.

Trellises
The familiar 'rustic' trellis is common enough but looks out of place in a contemporary setting and has only a limited life. Rather more crisp is heavy-duty squared trellis, although this will need regular maintenance to prevent rot setting in; this is difficult if it is covered in climbing plants.

As an alternative, think of using something altogether different: scaffold poles, set vertically about 15 cm (6 inches) apart, into concrete. Plug the tops with a thick wooden dowel and train a broad-leafed climber such as *Vitis coignetiae* or *Hedera colchica* 'Paddy's Pride' over the outline.

'Fedges'

A 'fedge' is a cross between a fence and a hedge, combining the good qualities of both. It is built by fixing heavy-duty plastic mesh between stout timber posts, spaced about 1.2 m (4 feet) apart, with galvanised staples. The height can be variable, depending on the setting. Climbers should be trained up and over the structure. If evergreen, they will give you cover throughout the year as well as flowers, and, unlike a hedge, they will only need occasional pruning to keep in check.

Of course such a technique can be modified to produce any number of shapes: within an area of ground cover, an 'ivy' garden perhaps, you could make up wire frames to simulate animals or rather more interesting geometric shapes. Such patterns make dramatic statements, particularly in winter, and could associate particularly well with a crisp modern façade, or perhaps a secret garden full of drama.

Hedges

Hedges span the gap between the hard elements of paving and walling and the softer backdrop of planting. They can form excellent divisions within the garden, as well as a tough sensible boundary that is capable of soaking up a remarkable degree of traffic noise and pollution. They can offer colour and interest throughout the year and, depending on the species, only need a single annual clipping. If you are keen enough, a hedge, or part of a hedge, can be clipped into a 'topiary' shape, forming a focal point. Topiary is a good deal cheaper and probably more attractive than the majority of sculpture available on the market.

Where fence panels or sections of fence are necessarily straight, hedges can be planted in a curve, something to bear in mind when building up the pattern of a garden. Nor need they necessarily be thought of in terms of screening: the smaller types, such as lavender, box or santolina, can define beds or paths at a much lower level, emphasising plants nearer the ground. Some types, such as pyracantha, holly or berberis have sharp spines, making them an ideal deterrent on a boundary, but remember that all hedges will take a great deal of nourishment out of the ground so will not only need regular feeding but also sound preparation (see page 93).

Your boundary is visible from inside and out. Because of that it not only sets the scene for the garden within; it should present a sympathetic face to the world outside as well. Any boundary should therefore be chosen with due regard to the overall budget available, the degree of on-going maintenance, the provision of shelter, the visual effect on the garden and the suitability of its public side. With a garden of reasonable size the financial outlay can be considerable, so choose carefully and remember that in landscaping you very much get what you pay for, both in terms of materials and labour.

HARD LANDSCAPE

By now you will have a good idea of what materials to use for the 'walls' of your outdoor room, as well as the composition and positioning of any screens within those boundaries.

The next step is to decide on the 'floor' coverings. These can be divided into the two main areas of paving and planting, or, as they are called in professional terms, 'hard' and 'soft' landscaping. The former I will discuss in this chapter, the latter in the next.

The hard landscape of a garden embraces all surfaces such as paving, paths, drives, hardstanding areas, decking, steps and ramps. As such, it very much constitutes the frame or skeleton of the whole composition, defining planted areas, providing room for sitting and dining and allowing dry-shod access around the garden. As I said in the last chapter, this element of the design may well account for up to 75 per cent of the total budget, so it will make sound sense to choose materials carefully, and to make sure that they are laid correctly to ensure a long life.

As with boundaries, there can be certain local building styles and traditions that could influence your choice; the most important of these are the ones that you have in your house, for instance, a stone-flagged floor inside is most effectively highlighted by a similar surface outside. And if adjoining garden walls are built from granite it is pretty incongruous to use a garish mixture of coloured pre-cast concrete paving slabs for the patio.

Where a boundary usually looks best built from a single material, the ample size of a terrace can provide a little more scope, allowing you to team two, or just occasionally more, materials together. This does a number of things: it prevents a single surface from becoming too visually 'heavy', and means there is an opportunity to build up an interesting combination of surfaces that can set the theme for hard landscaping throughout the garden. It is also worth bearing in mind that the terrace or patio is often the first point of contact with the garden at the rear of the house, and, likewise, hard-surfacing almost invariably sets the theme at the front. Because first impressions count, it will be all the more important to plan these areas with sensitivity and with practicality in mind.

How much room will you need?

On your rough plan you have broadly allocated areas for all the main features that you want in the garden. Now you need to firm these up and draw them to scale, so that you can not only accurately estimate the quantity of materials required, but see how the garden has evolved in terms of a satisfactory design that fits your own family needs.

As a general rule, a terrace or patio needs to be a minimum of 3.6 m (12 feet) square. This will allow adequate room for tables and chairs and thus avoid the disaster of you or your guests tip-

These tiles are an unusual and attractive hard surface for a town garden.

ping backwards into a flower bed followed by a cup of tea! If it is to provide ample play space, perhaps for a sandpit that can be easily swept up after use, and of course for wheeled toys, you may require an additional area.

Of course a terrace or patio will not exist in isolation and it will be sensible to site it within easy reach of the house, usually adjoining sliding or French doors. Link it to other parts of the building and garden as well. This will involve laying paths, which should be a minimum of 60 cm (2 feet) wide and ideally 120 cm (4 feet) wide. If a path adjoins a lawn it should be set slightly lower than the turf, thus acting as a mowing edge. It can also separate planting from lawn, and prevent leaves and blooms from being severed in their prime. Paths are also ideal for wheeled toys, but there is nothing more frustrating for a youngster than having to stop in full flight, so why not plan the route to continue right around the garden? It will make access for feet and wheelbar-

rows a lot easier, too, particularly in wet weather.

Another area for paving will be that allocated to sheds and garden buildings, not only for the base but as a surround. If possible, always allow approximately 1.8 m (6 feet) square outside the building, as this is where you will pause with a wheelbarrow or other equipment. It is also essential for a shed door to swing open without forcing you to step backwards into a bed or border.

Doing it yourself

Where some types of walling are best left to the professional, there is no reason why the average person should not be able to tackle most kinds of paving. I will deal with the individual laying techniques of different materials later on in this chapter, but a few basic rules apply to virtually all the work you are likely to carry out.

Perhaps the most important point to remember is that a paved area should be planned to last indefinitely; and that being the case thorough preparation is absolutely vital. It is also essential that the finished level is at least two courses of brick or 15 cm (6 inches) below the damp-proof course of your house. You can usually identify the damp-proof course by looking for a slightly wider course of brickwork, close to ground level; you may also be able to see signs of the bituminous strip that forms this vital waterproof layer.

If there is any likelihood of the paving being laid above or 'bridging' the damp-proof course, the ground must first be dug away to accommodate the foundation of the paving and the thickness of the slabs themselves.

Another vital rule is to ensure that the paving slopes away from the house so that water can run off into an adjoining bed or lawn area. The slope or 'fall' need not be great; 1 in 100 is ample. If the ground rises up away from the house there may well be difficulty in getting rid of surplus water, and in this case you may have to run it into a drain situated within the patio area and connected to a soakaway. It contravenes local building regulations to run surface water into the house drains. The location of a drainage gully may well fit into a paving pattern, perhaps at the junction of two courses of paving brick or at the centre of a neatly slabbed rectangle.

Choosing materials

A trip to any garden centre or builders' merchants will astonish you with the vast array of materials available. It may also confuse you, and because confusion is fatal to good design, you need to ask a few sensible questions to narrow the field and ensure a sensible end result.

Such questions revolve around the budget you have allocated for the job, what you want from the finished design, and, finally, the characteristics of the materials involved.

Cost

This can be broken down into two areas, the cost of the actual materials that you choose and the additional labour cost, should you decide to have a contractor carry the work out for you.

As far as the materials are concerned, man-made surfaces such as pre-cast slabs or concrete will be less expensive than, for example, natural stone. This is due in part to the long distances stone may have to travel from its quarry and of course the labour in getting it out of the ground and shaping it for domestic use. On the credit side, something like York stone lasts a lifetime and often mellows with age to give a garden the delightful charm of maturity.

It is also fair to say that small-scale materials like cobbles or granite setts take a lot longer to lay than a straightforward slabbed patio, and this will be reflected in any labour charges. The costs of a good landscape gardener are comparable to those of a good builder; just as with builders, you should not automatically accept the lowest price around without checking the quality of a firm's work. There are far too many 'cowboys' in garden construction and they are to be avoided at all costs. A recommendation from a friend would also be sensible.

The character of the materials

The size and shape of an area to be surfaced may well dictate what you choose. For instance, a sweep of drive will be cheaper and easier to lay in concrete, gravel or tarmac than in paving slabs. All the former are 'fluid', in that they can be cast or laid to a curved pattern; slabs would need to be cut to a curve, which is time-consuming and 'fussy' in appearance.

The surface texture will also have a bearing on what should be used in a given situation, in other words use smooth paving slabs or concrete for a path or patio that is likely to be frequently walked on and to be a base for tables and chairs. Cobbles bedded in cement or the uneven surface of granite setts tend to deter walkers, and in the right place are useful for that reason.

Design potential

Because of the wide range of materials, keep the layout as straightforward as possible; remember that simplicity is the key to good design. We have already seen, for example, that an ideal link between a brick house and garden is the use of a similar material for paving or walling.

It is also worth making the point that quite unlikely materials can make excellent paving. Railway sleepers, log slices, pre-cast concrete kerb edges – laid flat instead of on edge – and timber decking can all make interesting and durable surfaces. In other words, lateral thinking in the garden is essential; it can also make the best of the most unlikely bargain and save you a great deal of cash in the process!

Remember, too, that simply to copy ideas out of a book or from another garden rarely produces a satisfactory design. Find inspiration by all means, and certainly keep looking about you for fresh ideas. By doing this you will eventually come up with that unique composition with which you feel comfortable and satisfied.

Options for hard surfaces

Hard-landscaping materials fall into two main categories: man-man and natural surfaces. We shall look now at the many options in each category, beginning with the range of man-made surfaces.

Concrete slabs

There are an increasing number of pre-cast concrete paving slabs coming on to the market. Nearly all are reasonably priced and some are a very good imitation of natural stone, making them an ideal choice for many situations, particularly if the house is built from reconstituted stone. Some, however – and those that come in a range of garish colours spring immediately to mind – are not so attractive and tend to fade to a sickly hue after prolonged exposure to sunlight.

The surface texture can range from deeply furrowed or 'riven' to perfectly smooth: the former has a slightly rustic feel, and incidentally provides a better grip underfoot; the latter is rather more architectural, blending well into a modern setting. Slabs are available in a vast range of sizes, and, as with other areas of the design, try and keep things as simple as possible. Remember, your terrace or patio is a background for a wide range of activities and should not be a visual showstopper in its own right.

As a general rule, stick to a straightforward theme of using either a single size of slab or a random pattern that should imitate a terrace in natural stone flags. A square slab will give a more static appearance than a long rectangular shape and the latter can be used to lead the eye in a particular direction. If laid across a narrow space, they will help to open it up and make it seem wider. A deep joint between the slabs will help to emphasise the pattern.

Another use for paving may be as a coping, either on a garden wall or on a raised bed. In the latter case, this will not only double as a seat but provide visual continuity with the adjoining terrace.

Concrete slabs combined with brick are attractive and economical.

Paving slabs make excellent 'stepping stone' paths in grassy areas.

When slabs are wet they turn darker, something to bear in mind if you are flooring a shady basement or courtyard. In this case you might want to use a very pale slab, to reflect the maximum amount of light.

Of course, rectangles are not the only shapes available: hexagons and circles are common too. While these are often a little awkward close to the clean lines of a building, they can make excellent stepping stones and form an ideal informal sitting area in a more distant part of the garden. Also try and respect the underlying character of a material. Hexagons are a 'busy' pattern and there is little point in finishing an area paved with them in a straight line, as so often happens. Instead, use them as a path or terrace, where they can be run off into adjoining planting as a random edge.

Laying paving slabs
The method that you employ to lay paving slabs will determine not simply how long they will last, but how long they will remain as a durable, true surface.

The quickest, cheapest and least effective method, used by many builders around new homes, is simply to bed the slabs on a layer of sand. This will involve levelling the ground and compacting it either with a rammer of some kind or a heavy roller. Following this you should spread a layer of sand approximately 8 cm (3 inches) thick, and bed the slabs accordingly, butting the slabs tightly together. The disadvantage of this method is the ease with which the surface becomes undermined by rain and weather, even if the outside of the area is held firmly in place by an edging of some kind.

The second method, and the one that is most commonly employed, is to excavate the area (always remembering that the finished paving level should be 15 cm (6 inches) below the damp-proof course) and lay a well consolidated layer of crushed stone or hardcore approximately 15 cm (6 inches) thick. Cover or 'blind' this with a layer of ash or sand to fill in the cracks between the hardcore or stones. The slabs can then be positioned with five dabs of mortar, one at each corner and one in the middle. Slabs can either be butted closely together or laid with a joint, in which case you will need to employ wooden spacers that can be removed before you point the paving. Always work to a gentle 'fall' as mentioned earlier (page 55), and continually check your work with a long straight edge and a spirit level.

The third and final method is the most durable of all and would be suitable where a surface is subject to heavy traffic, on a drive perhaps. Here the preparation is the same as for the last

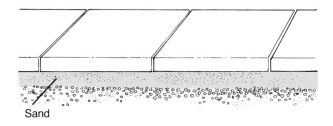

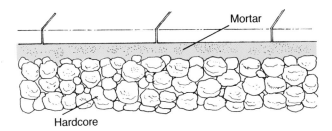

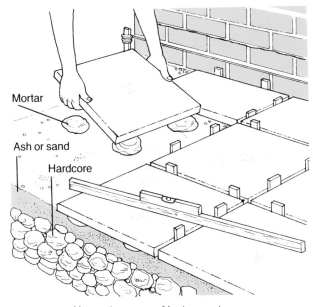

Alternative ways of laying paving.

method, but if the ground is soft make sure there is ample foundation, up to 30 cm (1 foot), if necessary. The slabs are then bedded on a continuous layer of mortar and either butt-jointed or pointed as before. The advantage of this technique is strength; the disadvantage is the difficulty of reaching any services beneath the area in times of emergency. Always bear in mind the position of drains, water pipes and electric cables when undertaking any work in the garden; check against builder's plans and look for the positions of manholes, stop-cock-covers and so on.

Instead of a continuous paved area, there is, of course, the possibility of laying paving slabs across a lawn or through a planted area as stepping stones. Where the former is concerned, a path will play an important part in the garden design, leading feet and eye across or through a space in a particular direction. The easiest way to lay the path out is by carefully scaling the line from your plan and setting this out on the ground. If the path is curved, locate the radius point and fix this with a peg or cane. A line can be swung that indicates the route of the path, this being easily marked with sand. Now set the slabs out by simply placing them on the lawn. Make sure the gaps between each are comfortable by walking the path. Once you are satisfied that all is well, slit around each slab with a spade or half-moon edging iron, lift the turf and bed the slab just below the level of the turf on a layer of sand or weak mix of mortar, making sure it is true by using a short spirit level.

Concrete paving blocks

These are approximately the same size as a brick and come in a range of colours; some are attractive, some, frankly, are awful. They are extremely durable (hence ideal for drives), resistant to frost and can be laid quickly; and as they have a chamfered edge they can be butt-jointed without pointing.

They should be laid over a firm base of well consolidated hardcore or crushed stone, this being followed by a 16 cm (6-inch) layer of sharp sand. Edge restraints for the area are essential; these could be either similar blocks set in concrete, or long boards firmly wedged in place. Level the sand carefully and then lay the blocks in position.

The best way to level and settle them is to use a 'plate vibrator', which can easily be hired. Lastly, brush sand into the joints and vibrate the surface again, to make sure it is secure.

Blocks can be laid in a variety of patterns, in the same way as bricks, and they can be cut to fit the edge of an area, either with a club hammer and bolster, or with a hydraulic block splitter, which can also be hired.

Although most blocks are rectangular there are a number of interlocking patterns available, and these are better used in a more informal part of the garden.

Brick paving

We have already seen that brick is an ideal material for walls, and it is no less effective used as paving. The major difference is that if it is used for the latter it must be able to withstand winter frost, which can quickly break the surface down and make it uneven. As a general rule, if you can flake the surface by twisting a coin hard then it will be too soft for garden paving use, and this can eliminate the old second-hand bricks that look so attractive in a builder's yard. Having said that, there are many suitable house bricks, and there are a number of manufacturers now producing bricks specifically for paving.

Brick paving almost invariably looks best in conjunction with another surface, pre-cast slabs or natural stone flags perhaps. In this rôle, it softens the overall surface and can of course be the perfect link with the adjoining building, should that too be brick-built. Used by itself in a large area, it can look a little heavy: the intimacy of each module being submerged by the overall mass of the surface.

While it is worth trying to match the tone of paving and house bricks, the former will tend to weather down to a slightly different and usually more mellow colour.

There are a number of brick paving patterns that include: 'stretcher bond', 'soldier courses', 'herringbone' and 'basketweave'. Each has its own character, and it is worth remembering that each, too, has a degree of visual emphasis that can be used to good advantage in the design. For instance, if a path is laid in 'stretcher bond' with the pattern running down the length of the path, this will lead the eye on and tend to foreshorten the space. This same bond laid across the path will do just the opposite, slowing things down and visually linking with features or planting to either side.

Bricks can be laid in a number of ways, the most common of which involves bedding them over hardcore on 5 cm (2 inches) of dry mortar mix, made up from four parts of soft sand to one part cement. Once the path or paved area is laid, brush more of the same dry mix into the open joints and let the moisture in the ground harden the mortar. Alternatively, carefully water the bricks with a spray, being sure not to wash any of the mortar on to the paving, where it would leave an unpleasant and unworkmanlike stain.

Some new pavers can be laid on 5 cm (2 inches) of sharp sand over 15 cm (6 inches) of hardcore. Consolidate with a 'plate vibrator', as described above. 'Restrain' the edges by bricks set in mortar or boards wedged securely in place.

'Stretcher bond' brick pavers used across
the path, visually broadening the space.

Two bands of 'soldier courses', alternating with
the bands of 'stretcher bond'.

'Herringbone' brick paving pattern,
edged with 'soldier courses'.

'Basketweave' brick paving, laid
on edge.

Stable pavers

If the area is likely to take heavy wear, you can bed the bricks on a wet mortar mix of the same strength and point the joints carefully.

Stable pavers
These were traditionally used for flooring stables and yards. They are about the same size as a brick but about half the thickness. They are very hard and the top surface is usually marked with either a diamond or a square pattern, to provide grip for hooves. You may find them for sale in demolition yards in dark blue or red. The nature of the surface makes them ideal for a driveway, or as dividing strips between other types of paving. Because they are somewhat uneven, they are not the best choice beneath tables and chairs.

Cast concrete
Paving slabs are obviously cast to a specific shape, but you can use concrete in altogether larger shapes and patterns, casting it on the spot. Such patterns will need to be carefully worked out at the design stage and could be built up in rectangular panels, divided by courses of paving,

wood strips or brick. Such dividers do more than just create a combination of surfaces, they act as 'expansion joints', preventing an area of concrete that is too large from cracking. The panels themselves should be a maximum of approximately 3.6 m (12 feet) square, and such a design could provide a most attractive patio or front garden, where paving could be interspaced with grass and planting.

It is also worth remembering that concrete can be cast to a free-flowing pattern, and this could make it ideal for a curved driveway or terrace. The surface can be treated in a number of ways while the concrete is still workable. A soft broom will produce gentle ribbing, while a board tamped across a path or drive creates positive ridges, useful for a non-slip finish. A steel float smooths the surface out flat; a wooden float leaves it slightly more rough.

Perhaps the best technique, and one that is widely used in the United States and on the Continent, is to wait until the surface is almost dry, and then spray it with water and carefully brush the concrete with a soft broom. This will expose all the small stones in the mix and the resulting 'marbled' finish is most attractive. It is a great shame that concrete is not used more in this country; it is inexpensive and highly versatile; all you really need is imagination.

Tarmac
Tarmac can be laid in two basic ways, as bitumen or asphalt. The latter is more commonly used in a domestic situation; bitumen is harder wearing and suitable for drives or heavy traffic areas. Bitumen is best laid by a reputable contractor, *not* one that calls 'on spec' with a load left over from your nearest motorway! If you have someone to do the job for you, keep the scheme simple and don't have it peppered with white chippings,

A crazy-paving path, edged with a strong, neat brick course to contain the complex, broken pattern.

which look awful. Similarly, keep clear of red and green bitumen, which either look like a tennis court or bring to mind a scene from the front garden of an American 'soap': both approaches are pretentious.

Asphalt is more suitable for domestic use. Available in bags, it is spread over a layer of hardcore that has been 'blinded' with sand or ash. Rake it out and roll immediately after laying; top-dress with gravel for an attractive finish.

Like concrete, tarmac can be laid in a free-flowing pattern, or contained within squares or strips. To avoid the usual black finish, use golden pea gravel as the top surface and roll it in.

There is an almost equally wide range of natural materials for paving available.

Stone
Natural stone is the finest and most expensive paving available. It can range from locally quarried sandstone to the more exotic slate or even marble.

York stone is widely known and used. It has considerable variations in colour, depending on exactly where it was quarried. Old York stone can come either as solid rectangular slabs, usually lifted from old pavements or mill floors, or as crazy paving. I have advised against using broken paving close to a house, but it can look a great deal better if it is carefully laid, pointed, and contained within a strong pattern of brick or slab squares. If choosing old York stone, make sure it is as clean as possible: it is sometimes contaminated with oil and this can 'sweat' out during hot weather, staining all that comes into contact with it. The thickness can vary considerably, from 5 cm (2 inches) to 13 cm (5 inches). Thick slabs are not only heavier than thin ones, but involve foundations of greater depth to make the finished surface level.

The weight of natural stone allows it to be bedded on a minimal foundation, and if the ground is firm it can often be enough to lay slabs on sifted soil. A random rectangular pattern is traditional,

Lay paving flags radiating from a central 'key stone'.

and some joints need not be pointed, allowing low-growing plants to be introduced. Similarly, small areas can be left between stones, to be filled with either brick paving or planting. When building up the paving pattern, try to stagger the joints; it can be helpful to start the work with a centrally placed 'key stone' and radiate the pattern out from that.

Natural stone is difficult to cut, but there is usually little need to lay the edge of a terrace or path as a straight line. Instead, allow the slabs to 'die off' into the adjoining lawn or planting as a random edge: it will look far more natural.

One of the drawbacks of natural stone is its tendency to become slippery, particularly in shady conditions. I would suggest scrubbing it once a year with either detergent or salt, to minimise the problem.

You can, of course, still obtain new York stone, but it is horrendously expensive and much lighter in colour than old stone. I feel it has little of the character of the old stone, and a good pre-cast concrete slab looks almost as attractive.

Slate
Slate is a crisp, architectural paving that can look superb in a contemporary setting. Because of its dark colour it would not be suitable in a shaded area, but teamed with a lighter material, such as gravel or white chippings, together with sculptural planting, the results can be stunning.

Marble
Marble has the opposite qualities to slate; it is shiny and garish in all but the most contrived setting. Marble can be employed in a municipal precinct for steps and paving, where it looks fine; used as crazy paving in a suburban front garden, it is awful. It is also incredibly expensive, which should, I hope, eliminate it from your consideration.

Granite setts
These were originally old street paving, but are now available both new and second-hand. Full

Granite setts

setts are about the same size as a brick; a half-sett is what the name implies. Being granite, setts are almost indestructible; and their small size means that they can be laid to a curve, as a feature surrounding a tree or other focal point. Being slightly uneven, they are not ideal for a patio beneath tables and chairs, but this same characteristic makes them a good choice for a path or drive, where grip is needed. They could also be used as dividing strips within an overall surface of some other paving. They should be laid on a bed of mortar over hardcore and packed together as tightly as possible, without pointing, so that no joints are visible.

Cobbles

When you visit a beach, those wonderful, smooth, round stones are cobbles. They are water-washed and polished and can look superb in the garden. Before you fill the boot of your car, though, remember it is illegal to take them from the seaside! Buy cobbles from stone merchants or garden centres.

Cobbles can be laid in a variety of patterns; coursed or uncoursed, swirls, circles or rectangles. Because of their uneven nature they are difficult to walk on, and this can be a useful deterrent to people cutting corners, particularly when teamed with a group of large, smooth boulders with planting, to provide sculptural emphasis. The photograph on page 47 shows how this can be done.

A practical suggestion is to incorporate cobbles into a drive area, in a position where a car stands regularly. Any oil drips will be disguised by the cobbles, whereas paving or another surface might show an unsightly stain.

Lay cobbles as closely together as possible, in a bed of mortar, avoiding the 'currant bun' method beloved by councils, in which the odd stone is displayed in a sea of cement. No joints should be visible and all the tops should be made absolutely

Cobbles

level by tamping them in place with a long, straight edge.

Cobbles can also be laid loose as an excellent ground cover; they associate well with planting and provide an interesting texture, particularly during the long winter months.

Gravel

Gravel is a versatile, relatively inexpensive and good-looking surface. It has a character that is rather less formal than paving but rather more so than grass; it associates particularly well with architecture; and it makes an ideal path or drive. In a very small garden where grass might be impractical, it can be used as the main flooring material and planting can be allowed to grow through the surface, which helps to soften the outline.

All too often it is poorly laid, which results in a tiresome treadmill to the front door: something to be avoided at all costs. To lay gravel properly, thorough compaction is needed at all stages of the job and it can be well worth hiring a mechanical vibrating roller to consolidate the work. Simple shapes and curves are easier on the eye and easier to work to than complicated ones.

As a base for a drive, use a minimum of 15 cm (6 inches) of crushed hardcore or stone, topping this with a 5 cm (2-inch) layer of 5 cm (2-inch) gravel, well rolled in. Next spread a 3 cm (1-inch) layer of fine gravel mixed with hoggin (a clay mixture available from the same source as the gravel), which acts as a binder. Finally top-dress the surface with 1 cm (⅜ inch) pea shingle, and roll it well in to produce a durable end result.

A stout edge is essential to prevent the surface from being undermined. This can be bricks laid end-to-end and firmly bedded or 'haunched' in concrete: they would be an expensive but superb finish. Alternatively, use boards treated with preservative, and firmly hold them in position

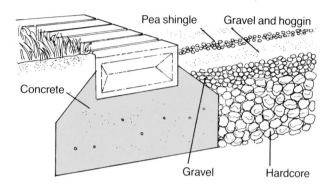

Gravel drives need secure edges if the surface is not to disappear after time.

with stout pegs. Try and resist the use of kerb edges, which look dreadful on a curve because they produce a hexagonal effect that is uncomfortable on the eye. If grass adjoins the area, make sure it is set 10 cm (4 inches) above the gravel, to minimise the chance of stones finding their way into cylinder mower blades.

Timber decking

This is a versatile material and an ideal do-it-yourself project; it is widely used in Scandinavia and the United States. Timber warms up quickly underfoot, is easy to cut and shape and does not need the more complicated foundations of other types of paving. In this country, always use either pressure-treated timber or wood that is painted with a non-toxic preservative. Ventilation beneath a deck is essential, and this will mean building the surface on to solid timber joists, these being bolted to posts set into the ground.

On a sloping site a deck can be ideal, making expensive retaining walls unnecessary and incorporating wide timber steps that extend the theme. Seating can be naturally linked into the pattern, and the surface can be neatly fitted around existing trees and other vegetation.

Railway sleepers make an extremely hard-wearing surface.

Timber decking is excellent for hard surfaces and steps.

When building a deck, always order slightly more timber than you need, so that you have a few boards left over. These will weather naturally if left outside and will make an ideal match if any replacements are needed.

Railway sleepers

These solid baulks of timber are still readily available, from British Rail or through the pages of *Exchange and Mart* or *Farmers Weekly*. They can make unusual and durable paving and look particularly good in an informal part of the garden. Try to select sleepers that are as clean as possible, because tar can sometimes seep from the surface during particularly hot weather. Because of their weight, foundations for sleeper paving need be only minimal; a bed of level sand is quite adequate.

To extend the theme, why not also use sleepers for raised beds? They should be laid in a staggered bond, like bricks; because they are heavy, make sure someone gives you a hand lifting them into position. If the sleepers are stacked more than three high, drill holes 30 cm (1 foot) from each end to accept lengths of steel rod that can be driven well into the ground as supports. Cutting sleepers is virtually impossible except with a chain saw, and if you use this kind of tool be aware of the dangers and take adequate safety precautions.

Sleepers will also make delightful and unusual steps. Use a staggered pattern up a bank, holding them firmly in place with wooden wedges, and allow planting to soften the edges and outlines.

Log slices are a delightful rustic alternative to paving stabs for 'stepping stones'.

Log slices

Hardwoods such as oak, elm and beech are ideal for use in the garden, because they are slow to rot. This is a good way to use timber that may have been blown down by high winds. Sliced into circular sections about 15 cm (6 inches) thick, they make excellent stepping stones through a planted area. If the slices become slippery, nail fine-mesh galvanised chicken wire on to the surface to provide better grip. When laying log slices across a lawn, make sure that they are set just below the level of the turf, for easy mowing.

Other aspects of hard landscape

As well as thinking of the 'floor' of your outside room, before going on to plan planting you should give some thought to a few other aspects of hard landscape.

Manholes

Manholes are an essential part of your drainage system, but, having said that, they aren't usually a welcome feature. They always seem to be in the most awkward position, often right outside the patio doors!

Although it may be tempting to cover them with concrete or paving, the temptation should be resisted. The best solution is to disguise the outline, which is almost inevitably set at an angle to the house and the paving pattern that you have so carefully worked out. If this angle is not too great it may be possible to lift the cover and turn it to match the line of paving, carefully bedding the rim back in mortar. Alternatively, you can buy 'recessed' covers, which accept a cut paving slab or suitable mix of concrete.

If the manhole is not in the middle of a paved area or path, cover it with loose cobbles and several smooth boulders, using spreading plants like

Raised beds create visual interest by introducing height to flat areas.

Cotoneaster horizontalis or *Juniperus × media* 'Old Gold', to soften the outline. It will be easy enough to roll the stones out of the way should you need access at any time.

A final thought: never cover a manhole with a pot or statue; this simply draws the eye, and emphasises rather than detracts from the problem.

Raised beds

Raised beds are enormously useful within a paved area, to soften a strong horizontal line and provide vertical emphasis. They can be built from virtually any of the materials we have discussed, and, as well as being easy to maintain without stooping, they give young plants an initial boost and much-needed height.

Their position can be worked out at the design stage: they might define the edge of a patio, or perhaps act as a pivot to the whole area, linking into an overall paving pattern. They can look most effective adjoining steps, softening the outline of a crisp, architectural flight. It is also worth remembering that the soil you put in a raised bed can be different to that found in the rest of the garden, meaning, for example, that you could introduce an acid soil, suitable for rhododendrons and azaleas, in a chalky or alkaline area.

Any raised bed is only a container, however, albeit a large one. This being the case, water raised beds regularly during dry weather and incorporate drainage holes at the bottom if necessary.

Steps

While many gardens are flat, many more are set on a slope and this offers all kinds of design opportunities. Where the style is informal, grassy slopes and gentle contours can be both effective and practical. In a more formal or architectural setting, however, steps will be the obvious choice. As far as dimensions are concerned, steps should never be mean. Not only will these look uncomfortable, they may well be dangerous. A useful guide says that the risers should be 15 cm (6 inches) high and the treads (the flat part) 45 cm (18 inches) deep. The width can be generous and in my own garden I have several gentle steps that are 3 m (10 feet) wide. This allows ample scope for a group of pots or a well chosen statue, which can act as a focal point.

These wide, very gentle steps give almost as much ease of access as would a ramp.

*Planting can be allowed to soften
even small, neat steps.*

When undertaking construction, always ensure that there is a slight slope on all the surfaces. This will shed water easily and prevent the build-up of potentially lethal ice during frosty weather.

If the flight is a long one, you should think of incorporating a landing every 15 steps or so. This is another opportunity for a group of pots, or you could leave a gap for planting that can soften an adjoining retaining wall. The direction of a flight could change at this point, through 90 or 45 degrees.

Of course, steps need not simply be a small part of a garden. On a scheme I recently completed I used steps as a series of hexagonal, interlocking platforms, fully 7.5 m (25 feet) across, which worked their way gently up a slope, occupying most of the available plot. Some were given over to grass, others to gravel and planting; one was large enough to double as a sitting area.

Steps can also be made from virtually any of the materials I have mentioned in this chapter. It can be useful on an easy-going flight to build the edge of the step from a different material to the rest of the tread, so that you have a visual 'warning' of the change in level.

Ramps
Steps can, of course, present problems to children as well as the elderly or disabled, and in this instance a gentle ramp, or a series of ramps, will be most welcome.

They will also be useful for moving garden machinery, as well as well laden wheelbarrows. Use a material that provides grip for construction, such as granite setts, ribbed concrete, or stable pavers.

A ramp can look most effective, and, incidentally, climb more gently, if it is set to a curving pattern, or alternatively works its way diagonally across a slope.

SOFT LANDSCAPE

We can now see that the structure of the garden, in 'hard landscape' terms is vital not only to define the various areas or 'rooms', but to provide space for sitting, dining, access, play, utility and much much more. These elements provide the 'bones' of the composition, but by themselves they are bound to be both basic and austere.

To most people 'planting' *is* a garden, although we already know that there is far more to a successful garden design than that. It is this element, however, that will soften and surround the design, putting flesh on to those 'bones' and breathing life into the basic pattern.

The term 'planting' does, however, embrace a number of aspects, and we shall be looking at the positioning of shrubs, trees and herbaceous material in the next chapter. Such material will only occupy part of the pattern, and altogether larger areas may well be given over to grass and 'ground-covering plants', the latter forming an alternative carpet of a rather different kind to grass.

Lawns

A lawn should never be thought of simply in terms of something to fill in the gaps between all the other garden features and areas. Its purpose is in fact to unify those elements, pulling the design together into a coherent whole and leading feet and eyes through the composition as a restful backdrop. Apart from this it should be functional in its own right, playing host to a wide range of activities that range from family play, sitting and dining to access to the planted areas and other features that it adjoins.

Shapes
The shape of a lawn will obviously have a great influence on the overall garden design. An interlocking pattern of rectangles, perhaps linked or crossed by a pergola or trellis and backed up with planting, will be rather more static than free-flowing shapes that sweep around and through a garden. Both approaches are valid; choose the one that best relates to the underlying design theme that runs throughout the composition as a whole.

When working out those shapes keep them simple, avoiding awkward corners and angles that will be difficult to maintain. This is the time to think back to the chapter on design, where I suggested that you should use a pair of compasses for working out strong, flowing curves (page 25). These will naturally detract from rectangular boundaries, providing continuity and purpose. The more fussy shapes achieved by following the tortuous line of a hose pipe or washing line laid out at random on the grass will be far less effective! This is the time to think of the possible advantages of a path around the lawn, which will act as a mowing edge and provide access for maintenance such as weeding.

Rectangular shapes for borders and lawns give a structured feel to the garden.

Curved shapes for borders and lawns give a more fluid feel.

Slopes

Grass can, of course, grow on very steep banks, but here the real problem is in being able to mow it. A gentle slope is fine, and can often be a delightful link between different parts of the garden. For all practical purposes, a slope of more than 25 degrees is difficult for any kind of mower, although it is just possible to mow a bank of 45 degrees with a hover-type mower attached to a rope and worked across the slope. Such techniques are not ideal in a domestic garden, and can be dangerous if a machine gets out of control. If you have such a steep slope, ground-covering plants, which we will discuss a little later, are the ideal choice, because they will need little maintenance once established.

Quality

There is a lot of nonsense talked about the quality of turf or seed you should use; and there is also a lot of money spent on trying to keep an unsuitable lawn in top condition. What the average family most needs is a hard-wearing surface that will withstand maximum activity over as much of the year as possible. I don't mind a sprinkling of daisies in my lawn: the world would be a poorer place if children were prevented from making daisy chains! Speedwell, with its gem-like blue flowers, although invasive, also dots my own lawn, and, as long as neither takes over, I'm not too concerned. Of course, if you love a lawn and are prepared to spend time and money keeping it in tip-top condition, there is a range of fine seed mixtures and top-quality turves that will repay the initial outlay.

If you use turf, be careful if offered 'meadow' quality. This is just what it says and is cut straight from the field. It is certainly the cheapest available, but ensure it is treated against weeds because it may well be full of perennial species that will quickly multiply once the lawn is laid.

It is also worth bearing in mind that it is very difficult in a rural area to keep a lawn free from weed. Seed is continually blowing in from the surrounding countryside, and it may well be better to accept this rather than vainly trying to achieve a bowling green.

Laying a lawn with turf

Turf can provide an almost instant lawn, which is ideal for the average family garden. It can be established in as little as six weeks but it will be well worth the effort of keeping off the surface as much as possible during that time, certainly for hard-wearing play.

A great advantage is that turf can be laid at virtually any time of the year, as long as the ground

Laying turf: work from boards to avoid damaging the turves.

is not bone-dry, waterlogged or solid with frost. Good preparation is essential, and that will include thorough cultivation and the removal of stones, hardcore and perennial weeds. The soil should be broken down to a fine tilth and raked out to the finished levels. A granular fertiliser such as Growmore can be incorporated, to give the new grass a good start in life.

Turves should be laid like bricks in a wall, with staggered joints, and you should work from long planks or scaffold boards positioned on the row that you have just laid. Butt the sections together and firm them into position with a tamper made from boards set on the end of a handle. If you are working on a relatively steep slope, it can be useful to hold the turves in position with short wooden pegs, removing these once the roots have established.

If the weather is dry, regular irrigation of the turf is essential to ensure root development and to prevent it from shrinking so gaps appear. Should you see any gaps, brush in a mixture of sifted soil, peat and sand, again working off boards to minimise damaging the surface.

Instead of trying to lay turf to a curve, lay a little more than the area you need and cut the shape out with a sharp spade or half-moon edging iron, to form a crisp edge.

Growing a lawn from seed

The advantage of using seed is that you can select the blend of grasses that make up the lawn. Thus you could use a mixture that produces a luxury lawn, which will be largely made up from two types of grass known as 'fescues' and 'bents', while a hard-wearing utility lawn will probably contain a percentage of perennial rye-grass; the best seed mixes use the new shorter-leaved dwarf varieties of the latter. You can also sow a seed mix that is tolerant of a degree of shade, obviously useful under a (not-too-dense) tree canopy or in the shadow of buildings.

Prepare the ground in the same way as for turf, except that you will need to break the final surface down to a very fine tilth, removing as many stones as possible. To produce a successful lawn you will need a minimum of 15 cm (6 inches) of good-quality topsoil.

After carrying out the final grading, just check that you still have a sufficient depth of topsoil; then tread the whole area over to firm the ground down. Your final job will be to apply a pre-seed fertiliser, such as Growmore, and lightly rake this in.

As far as timing is concerned, the best times to sow seed are spring or early autumn; the summer is generally too hot for adequate irrigation and in winter the length of daylight and the lower temperatures prohibit good germination. If sowing in spring, it will be an excellent idea to carry out preparation during the previous autumn; if thinking of an autumn sow then prepare the ground in spring.

Maintaining a lawn

One of the most tiresome chores in the garden is hand-edging lawns. There are a number of tools that can make the job a good deal easier, but it is a very good idea to think of positioning a path right around the area. Not only will this provide access for feet, wheelbarrows, equipment and wheeled toys; it will also act as a 'mowing edge'. To do this, set the path slightly lower than the lawn so that the mower can run smoothly over the top. All that is then necessary is a once-yearly neatening-up with a sharp spade or edging iron. Another advantage is that by separating lawn and adjoining border you overcome that annoying tendency to trim off leaves and cherished blooms when mowing.

A solid lawn edge helps reduce maintenance.

A further problem arises when a lawn adjoins a building or retaining wall. Here there is a tendency for the mower either to hit the wall or to leave a strip of unmown grass. The answer is to set a row of bricks on edge, or a row of small slabs, against the wall. Make sure that they are positioned just below the turf, thus separating the horizontal and vertical surfaces.

Types of mower

The time was when you could buy only a push-along type or a more expensive petrol machine. In fact, I have a glorious advertisement, produced around the turn of the century, showing a steam mower. Getting it started and keeping it under control must have been quite something for the gardener at the forefront of technology!

However, today things are very different and there is a wide range of manual, petrol and electric machines available. A further choice will be between the traditional cylinder blades and the newer rotary types. The latter on the whole are more versatile, being able to tackle grass of different heights. However, unless they are fitted with a roller you will not get that 'banded' effect that so many people like to see on their lawn. This is simply caused by the grass being pushed one way on the way out, and the opposite on the way back.

Electric machines are safe, usually lightweight and efficient, and often ideal for today's smaller garden. If you have more than 15 m (50 feet) or so, the length of cable can become cumbersome and it can be worth thinking of a petrol-driven mower.

Rough grass areas

In a larger garden there can be areas where it is both practical and attractive to leave the grass rather longer, under fruit trees or in an informal area, for example. This being the case you will only need to cut infrequently: once after the spring bulbs have died down; again when the summer wild flowers have set their seed; and a final trim to put the area 'to bed' for winter. Bulbs and wild flowers are most attractive in this kind of setting and can be an ideal link with the landscape if you have a rural garden.

As far as paths are concerned it can be delightful simply to mow a route, or a number of routes, through the space, perhaps pausing at an informal sitting place before returning to the more structured part of the composition. The picture opposite shows how this can be done.

A simple and attractive path for a grassy area can be made by mowing.

Lawn care calendar

January
Little to do this month. Remove any leaves. Keep off the turf in freezing and waterlogged conditions.

Overhaul mowers and other lawn maintenance equipment.

February
Worm casts can start to be a problem. Remove these with a broom when they are dry.

March
The grass really starts to grow this month. As soon as the weather is reasonably dry, rake the lawn to remove leaves and other debris. A light rolling helps to compact any areas lifted by frost. Use a cylinder mower, if you have one, with the blades set high.

Two cuts are sufficient this month; never cut too close, keep the blades set high. Cut on a dry day.

Disease may start to be apparent. Moss-killer or worm-killer can be applied, strictly to manufacturer's recommendations.

April
Start to feed the lawn this month, and also to apply weed-killers (or a combination of both). However, only do this if the grass is growing strongly. In a late spring this may not be until later in the month.

If using lawn sand, spread it evenly and rake out the dead moss two weeks later.

Mow two or three times, with the blades set at 4 cm (1½ inches).

Seeding can be carried out this month.

May
Cut the lawn at more frequent intervals and reduce the height of the blades to 3 cm (1¼ inches). Once a week is usually necessary.

This is an ideal time for lawn treatment with selective weed-killers or lawn sand. When applying these, the weather should be dry and the ground moist. Do not apply in windy conditions.

If there is a drought – and this can occur this month – make sure to water regularly.

June
Reduce the blades to 2.5 cm (1 inch) and cut at least once a week. If the weather is particularly dry, set the blades a little higher and keep watering.

Summer feeds and weed-killer can be applied.

Apply a nitrogen-based feed to improve the colour of the lawn and increase vigour.

Edge trimming is important to keep things neat. If dry weather has set in, just spike the lawn with a fork to allow irrigation to sink in easily.

July
The height of summer, and often holiday time; if you can arrange for someone to cut the grass while you are away, so much the better. Keep the blades set at 2.5 cm (1 inch) and irrigate if dry weather.

Rake before mowing to raise clover stems so that they are severed.

August
This is the latest month for weed-killing, as growth has slowed down considerably.

If the grass has grown long after a holiday, simply 'top' the lawn initially, reducing this to 3 cm (1¼ inches) for the subsequent cuts.

You can start to sow seed this month.

September
This is the busiest lawn month, the blades should now be set at 3 cm (1¼ inches), and cutting should only be once a week, or even once a fortnight if growth is minimal.

Raking with a specialised lawn rake is the most important job, and after this any compacted areas should be aerated by spiking. Once this is carried out, a top dressing is really beneficial; make it from two parts sand, four parts loam, and one part peat. Spread this evenly and make sure it is worked down to ground level, rather than left on the leaves.

A combined fertiliser/weed-killer can be applied to prevent disease and boost the root system.

This is the best month for sowing a lawn.

October
This is the last regular mowing month. Apply combined fertiliser/weed-killer, if this was not done last month. Remove fallen leaves, twigs and general debris, which will be detrimental if left for any length of time.

A moss-killer can be applied this month.

November
If the weather has been mild it may be necessary to carry out the last cut. Do this if the ground is dry and frost-free.

Once this is done, overhaul all equipment; better to do it now than in a rush in the spring!

December
Put your feet up and enjoy the festive season. Simply brush off leaves, otherwise keep off the grass, particularly if wet or frozen.

Other types of lawn

Grass is not the only type of 'lawn' that you can have, although it is undoubtedly the hardest wearing. Certain other plants can also form a carpet and some of them need a good deal less maintenance.

Moss
If you look at a shady woodland area you will often see a soft carpet of moss, which naturally thrives under dark conditions in poorly drained soil. This is precisely why it invades poorly tended lawns. The Japanese have cultivated moss gardens or areas of this plant in the garden for many hundreds of years. While it is difficult to plant moss as a total ground cover it can be well worth encouraging it to run in an area where little else can grow and perhaps where it already has a hold. It will not take a great deal of wear but stepping stones through an area will provide access.

Thrift (Armeria maritima)
This is a ground hugging plant that forms tight clumps. It is impervious to the ravages of salt spray and this could make it ideal in a sunny seaside garden. Because it is uneven, it would be difficult to walk on; stepping stones would, again, solve the access problem. An area floored with this plant, in conjunction with smooth boulders, would form a sculptural element in its own right. Thrift is widely available from many nurseries and has pretty pink or white flowers during mid summer.

Thyme (Thymus serpyllum)
One of the most attractive 'lawns' I have seen used this delightful prostrate plant. The stronger growing varieties are about 5 cm (2 inches) tall and form mats up to 60 cm (2 feet) across. The leaves are strongly aromatic when crushed but too many feet would quickly destroy the surface. A sunny position is essential and flowers range through white, pink or red, depending on the variety.

Chamomile (Anthemis nobilis 'Treneague')
Many people have heard of a chamomile lawn but

few really know what it is or what it entails. Chamomile is a small, fragrant, clump-forming herb. The best type, the variety 'Treneague', is the one to use for a lawn. It does not flower and once established needs no cutting. It cannot withstand heavy wear and is therefore not a substitute for grass but for a small, perhaps formal area, it can be most attractive. Thorough preparation is essential and all perennial weeds must be removed. It is also worth bearing in mind that if any weeds do appear they will have to be removed by hand, as no mowing is carried out! Chamomile is in fact a 'ground-covering' plant, and we can now discuss these in more detail.

Ground cover

Ground cover is generally thought of as low, ground-hugging planting that is capable of smothering weed growth and that is usually positioned below taller-growing material. In fact many larger plants can act as ground cover in their own right and one has only to think of a dense rhododendron or large spreading juniper to see that they too can effectively exclude all growth underneath them.

The smaller ground-covering plants should be used in drifts rather than small clumps. This not only provides better density – out-competing those weeds! – but also gives the overall composition continuity. We shall be looking at planting design and the way in which plants can be related to one another in the next chapter, but it is important to underline the fact that all plants should be chosen primarily for their suitability in a particular situation. In other words, a sweep of ivy in a shady area overhung with trees will survive and flourish, whereas a similar drift of say *Salvia officinalis* (sage) will fail. The former enjoys shade; the latter, sun.

It is also important to see how one plant can enhance another. The traditional use of ground-hugging heathers together with conifers underlines the point that different shapes associate extremely well; the upright conifers provide the perfect foil for the hummocky heathers. On a rather larger scale, the arching sprays of *Cytisus kewensis* will be all the more telling in front of *Phormium tenax*, the New Zealand flax.

Many climbers make most attractive ground cover. They will run along a horizontal surface until they find something in the way, at which point they will revert to their more usual habit. Such plants thus serve a dual purpose, as ground cover and as cladding for unsightly tall objects. Suitable climbers for ground cover are honeysuckle, ivy and climbing hydrangea.

Many ground covers are evergreen, and as such will be able to provide colour and interest throughout the year.

Ground cover should not be allowed to invade other plants – this epimedium needs cutting back.

A fear that many people have is of the invasive nature of some of these plants, and it is quite true that if, say *Hypericum calycinum* (Rose of Sharon) is planted amongst more choice specimens, it will quickly take over and be almost impossible to remove. On a hot, dry, sunny bank on which little else will survive, however, this same plant can flourish. In shade, ivy and *Lamium galeobdolon* (dead nettle) are very similar; a pest in the wrong place where they choke less vigorous plants; a boon if you want to cover a single area with just one sturdy plant. If planted wisely, ground cover is a vital part of your garden's attractiveness and it reduces maintenance to a minimum. It can be kept in check by the quite ruthless use of a spade and can usually be propagated by simply chopping up the plants into pieces and replanting them.

By their very nature, ground-covering plants produce a blanket of foliage and help to smother weed growth. It is important however to prepare the ground thoroughly before planting to ensure that all perennial weeds are removed that could prevent the new planting from developing effectively. It will also be helpful to improve the ground at this stage, by the incorporation of as much organic matter as possible and also a slow-release fertiliser.

Maintenance with ground-covering plants is minimal, and that is, of course, one of the reasons they are used. If planted under trees, all species will benefit from the removal of fallen leaves that will discourage healthy growth. Some varieties – heathers are a particularly good example – benefit from clipping over in spring, to encourage dense growth. Like any plants, ground-covering plants benefit from regular feeding. Because it can be difficult to dig in organic material where there is a dense cover of foliage and stem, a liquid feed, applied during the spring and summer, will be ideal to encourage growth.

Annual plants as ground cover
Annual plants by their very nature are not hardy, and do not therefore last from one year to the next. They are not a 'true' ground cover in the way of low-growing shrubs and perennials; they can, however, be most useful for filling in gaps between shrubs in the general borders, as the latter develop and knit together. They are more labour-intensive because new plants need to be put in every year and of course they need clearing away after the frosts have killed them.

Virtually all of the lower-growing annuals would be fine, including lobelia, salvia, alyssum, petunias, nasturtiums, stocks, begonias and so on.

You can grow bedding plants from seed, or buy them as individual plants from your local garden centre. Only plant them after the last frosts are over, usually in late May.

PLANTS AND PLANTING DESIGN

By now you have an excellent idea of what you want in your new garden and have a pretty good idea of how it will look. In the previous chapter we discussed the role of low-growing ground cover plants; these act in much the same way as a carpet inside the house, covering the floor in a variety of colour and texture. Taller planting will take the composition into the 'third dimension', bring the garden alive and provide an ever-changing pattern of interest throughout the year.

In designing the various hard landscape elements you will have created a framework: allocating areas where shelter and screening is needed; positioning raised beds; leaving space for a herb garden; defining the size and shape of borders that surround lawns with paths; and allocating positions for trees that will provide vertical emphasis.

By now you should have learnt to resist the urge to rush out and have a buying binge at your nearest garden centre; the planning of planting is no less important than that initial choice of paving, walling or any of those other carefully selected and sited features.

What can you grow?

Whereas choice of hard landscape was largely dictated by local traditions, the immediate surroundings, and the budget available, similarly there are a number of important factors that will affect what plants are used in a particular part of the garden.

Where do you live?
Although Britain is a relatively small country, there is a considerable range of climatic conditions and this will have a marked influence on what you can grow, for example, areas in the north of the country have colder average temperatures than those in the south. This can mean that at a given time of the year, say spring, growing conditions prevailing in the north can be up to a month behind those in the south. Some plants are more 'tender', or less able to tolerate cold, frosty weather than others; seaside conditions with salt spray will also eliminate many species, while strong winds bring their own problems. In this country, average temperatures tend to reduce as one moves northwards; this is not a hard and fast rule because the warm waters of the Gulf Stream mean that large areas of the west coast of Scotland are virtually frost-free, allowing an unusually wide range of plants to be grown there.

When moving into a new area, it's a good idea to wait for a while before embarking on the design and construction of your garden. Ask local gardeners and perhaps your local Horticultural Society what unusual conditions prevail, and keep your eyes open to see what flourishes where.

All these local conditions add up to what we call a 'microclimate' and contribute to a local weather or climatic pattern that can be quite different from the national average.

Wind conditions

In our initial survey we looked at the possibilities of a prevailing wind or chill draught that might blow from a particular direction (page 11). Such a wind can be a real problem, stunting vegetation and drying out young plants to the point at which they fail altogether. A solid wall or fence is not always a good solution to this problem, because the wind strikes the barrier, swirls over the top and creates particularly unpleasant, turbulent conditions on the other side. Instead it is far more effective to plant a permeable screen of tough shrubs that can filter the wind and reduce its force. Any of such species as *Prunus laurocerasus, Viburum tinus, Ligustrum ovalifolium* and *Eleagnus ebbingii* would be ideal, providing shelter for the garden as a whole, as well as for the lighter and more colourful material that will be planted in its lee. If the garden is of a reasonable size a conifer hedge can do an excellent job, but remember that it will also grow extremely fast, need regular clipping, cast shade and take a great deal of nourishment from the ground.

The effectiveness of a well planted, tough screen of shrubs in giving shelter can be up to ten times its height measured in a lateral direction across the garden. The stronger the wind, the more gently the shelter belt should be graded so that the effects of turbulence are kept to a minimum.

Shade

Failure, more than any other single factor, turns people off gardening. Just what to plant in shade presents real problems to many people and to be

Many plants such as rhododendrons, hostas and astilbe can thrive in shade.

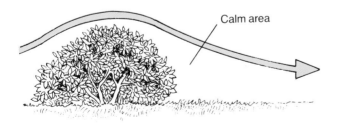

A permeable shrub screen filters the wind.

Calm area

fair there are a great many plants that are not happy in darker conditions. On the other hand you have only to look around at the natural world to see just how many species flourish under such circumstances; your garden is no exception.

In the country, trees are the major element in casting shadow; in town, buildings, fences, walls and a host of other structures add to the problems. Remember, too, that winter shadows are considerably longer than summer ones, when the sun swings higher in the sky. This is something worth noting on your initial survey and you can mark simple lines on the plan to indicate the difference between the two extremes. While some trees, such as sycamore and chestnut, cast very dense shade, making planting beneath them very difficult, others do quite the opposite, and can overshadow a good collection of the right kind of shrubs and herbaceous material without detrimental effect. Silver birch and mountain ash are good examples of the latter type.

Another problem with trees is the fact that they tend to shield the ground from heavy rainfall, and they also extract a good deal of nourishment from the soil. These are two more factors that will determine your choice of trees and point towards regular applications of organic matter and fertiliser around the trees and the plants near them (see page 111).

Many fine foliage plants are the answer for shady areas, and these can also provide an excellent background for more colourful plants that can be planted further away from the source of the shade. Such shrubs as *Fatsia japonica,* arundinaria, ligustrum, pyracantha, aucuba, sarcococca and mahonia will all be fine if planted in shade. Bergenia, ajuga, epimedium, hellebore and lamium are just a few of the hardy perennials, useful at a lower level, that will also help to solve your problems.

Frost

In microclimatic terms frost can present real problems, and these may not necessarily conform to a national pattern. Many gardens at the base of or part-way down a hillside are in a dip that holds the cold air; this is often referred to as a 'frost hollow'. A long wall or block of flats can similarly prevent cold air draining away, and you may not be able to grow tender species under such conditions. In some instances you can open a gap in a hedge or leave a space under a fence to allow this colder air to drain away to a lower level naturally.

Some years there are extremely hard winters, much more severe than the national average. This may mean that not only tender species but also more hardy types suffer. If the ground is frozen solid around roots for any length of time, death is not uncommon. Trees can display a delayed reaction to this; they come into leaf in the spring but then die later in the year. It is prudent to wait a while in the spring before removing seemingly dead plants, even if they appear to have been killed down to ground level. Plants are remarkably tough and you may find that after a

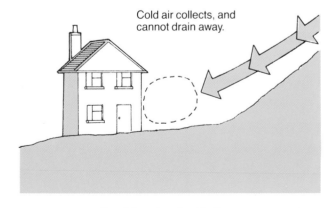

Cold air collects, and cannot drain away.

Conditions in a frost hollow

few weeks new shoots will appear and healthy growth resumes.

Traffic fumes
The effects of traffic fumes present a great problem, particularly in an urban area. Some plant species are more tolerant of fumes than others. Of the trees, chestnut and plane are a good choice, provided you have ample space; such shrubs as aucuba, fatsia, skimmia and privet also do remarkably well.

The need for screening
We have discussed the problems of noise earlier in the book (page 11), but it is worth reiterating that a contoured bank, heavily planted, will soak up a surprising amount of sound, perhaps from a road or adjoining playground. Suitable shrubs for screening are: *Eleagnus ebbingii*, privet, *Viburnum tinus*, aucuba, *Prunus laurocerasus* or *Prunus lusitanica*.

We also looked earlier at the question of what you can do to disguise a bad view. The problem may be caused by either distant or near-at-hand objects, the latter might include dustbins, a rickety garage or perhaps an unsightly oil tank. Sometimes it will be possible to build a physical screen in brick or timber, but if this proves impossible then a strong-growing climber, such as Russian vine, *Clematis montana* or the large-leafed evergreen ivies, will be invaluable. These can be trained over a trellis, or over plastic mesh that is firmly stapled to a timber framework.

Preparing the ground

We have already looked at the importance of preparing the site, including both lawn and planted areas (pages 31–8). It is absolutely vital that young plants are given the best possible chance and this will be made a great deal easier if the ground is well dug, well manured and well drained.

If the top soil is very poor or non-existent then you will need to bring some in, bearing in mind that shrubs and herbaceous material will need a depth of approximately 30 cm (12 inches) and a lawn about half that amount. If you are importing soil, always check the quality before it is tipped off the lorry: few drivers will shovel it back on again! If it is clearly substandard, perhaps with a good deal of sticky sub-soil, or if it is full of perennial weed such as dock or couch grass, then reject it.

Remember also that the type of soil you buy may be different from that found locally. In other words, you could have a load of acid or alkaline (chalky) soil. Always carry out a simple soil test before buying topsoil, because it isn't a good idea to mix the types, except when creating a special area, for example, a heather bed. The price of topsoil may also vary considerably, so it can be worth shopping around various garden centres or building sites where surplus soil might be for sale.

Planting design

The basic design of your garden can be likened to the way in which you arrange furniture in a room and most people could tackle this task with reasonable flair. The choice of plants can present rather different problems, however. Many would-be gardeners feel their real difficulties start here; all those Latin names, deciding what grows best where and estimating the eventual size of the plants you choose are just a few of the variables to take into account in making up the total pattern that we call planting design.

It is also fair to say that furnishing a room gives reasonably instant results, while plants take

These well stocked borders include acer, foxgloves, nicotiana, rogersia and marguerites.

rather longer to become established. In fact the question I am asked more often than any other is 'how long will it be before my garden is mature?' In all honesty, if you are using standard garden centre plants, it will take about five years for the borders to fatten up and for the composition to look at its best.

Of course you can mass plants together to give instant effect and you can also buy expensive 'semi-mature' material that will do the same thing. This is hardly cost-effective, however, and

will almost certainly involve removing many plants after a relatively short time.

A better approach would be to mix slower-growing shrubs with quickly maturing types such as broom, mallow, buddleia and forsythia. The latter are also relatively short-lived, and can be removed as the slower, more permanent shrubs knit together.

You can also fill the gaps between developing permanent planting with half-hardy annuals, which provide instant colour but do, of course, need to be replaced every year when they are killed by the winter frosts.

The use of colour

The British have long been considered to be a nation of gardeners, but just occasionally, usually once in each generation, a particular person excels at that particular craft. Around and after the turn of this century, Gertrude Jekyll had just such a talent, and, together with the architect Sir Edwin Lutyens, she created some most memorable compositions, which have influenced garden design up to the present day with her use and handling of colour in the garden. Of course the gardens on which she worked were far larger than today's suburban plot or small backyard, but the principles remain the same.

Gertrude Jekyll was initially a painter of no small talent and a great admirer of the Impressionist school. When her eyesight began to fail, she turned increasingly to gardening and applied many of the rules she used in creating canvasses to the colour groupings of plants in the garden. In broad terms, she stated that the 'hot' colours such as red, orange and yellow should be planted together, while the cooler and softer blues, pinks, purples and whites, along with all the other pastel shades, should be thought of as another combination.

Hot, vibrant colours have the effect of drawing the eye, and if placed at some distance from a view-point, demand instant attention, to the detriment of all else. This tends to foreshorten a space. To prove it, just place a tub of bright red pelargoniums at the bottom of your garden and see how they 'demand' your attention! The rest of the garden may well be built up from a number of other focal points and have a worthwhile underlying pattern, but that hot colour will cause instant disruption. The answer that Miss Jekyll suggested was to keep those vibrant colours close to the house or to the main viewpoint, fading away gradually with the softer hues that will naturally enhance a feeling of space and distance. Grey, as in many areas of design, acts as a harmoniser, linking colour-ranges together. In a country garden, where there is a view of the landscape, you can grade your colours and planting scheme so that it is almost impossible to see where garden and landscape adjoin.

Certain colour combinations are sure winners, purple and grey, for instance, or blue and white. Don't forget that foliage colour can be as important as flower so *Cotinus coggygria* 'Royal Purple' will look superb next to *Senecio greyii*, as will dark-blue delphiniums with pure white stocks or gypsophila.

Single-colour plant groups: shades of yellow and orange create a stunning effect.

Orange tulips make a dramatic highlight.　　　*Single-colour plant groups: shades of deep pink and mauve.*

Some gardens, or parts of gardens, can be planned with single colour-ranges in mind. Both Sissinghurst in Kent and Hidcote Manor in Gloucestershire are classic examples of this. On a smaller domestic scale, you might think of trying a similar idea in a long narrow garden, where the space can be divided into a series of 'rooms', each with a similar colour-range or theme. It can also be most effective to group certain plants of one colour. Roses are an excellent example, if not in one colour, certainly in the same colour-range. Drifts of annual bedding plants can be treated in much the same way, but do try and use drifts rather than the serried ranks like soldiers that some parks still display!

It is worth bearing in mind that all rules are made to be broken; while the above is a very sensible guide, there is no harm in injecting a splash of colour from a different range to add a point of emphasis. Take, for instance, that delightful spring flowering hardy perennial *Geum borisii*, with its vibrant red flowers. A ripple of such plants in a cool border is the same as a crisp highlight in a still-life painting. Another example might be the use of the blue grass *Festuca glauca* in front of the handsome leaves of the purple-leaved sage *Salvia officinalis* 'Purpurascens'. Plant shapes are another area to be exploited in order to give emphasis. For example the low, arching line of *Cytisus kewensis* works well against the counterpoint of yucca or phormium.

Making a planting plan

The great value of working to a plan is the fact that you can then implement the work over a period of time. This applies to both the 'hard landscape' elements that we have already discussed and the 'soft landscape' of plants. A plan also allows you to envisage how the garden or borders will look when complete, and it is far easier, cheaper and quicker to make corrections or modifications on paper than in the garden itself.

It is best to keep the main design plan and the planting plan separate, because to try and cram everything on to one drawing makes it far too complicated. The easiest way to work is to lay a sheet of tracing paper over the plan, and trace off the shapes of beds and borders; then fill in the plants on photocopies of the tracing.

Grouping plants

The problem with many gardens is that plants

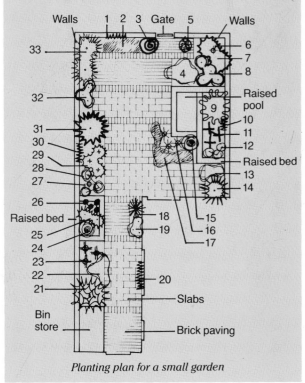

KEY
1 Clematis montana 'tetra rose' (1)
2 Geranium endresii (3)
3 Euonymus foetunei 'Silver Queen' (1)
4 Alchemilla mollis (4)
5 Annuals in pot
6 Robinia pseudoacacia Frisia (1)
7 Arundinaria nitida (2)
8 Helleborus corsicus (4)
9 Hydrangea macrophylla Blue Wave (1)
10 Lonicera serotina (1)
11 Skimmia japonica foremanii (3)
12 Hosta Thomas Hogg (3)
13 Astilbe Fanal (3)
14 Ceonothus Autumnal blue (1)
15 Dryopteris felix mas (1)
16 Anemone japonica (3)
17 Geranium Russell Pritchard (7)
18 Hebe rakaiensis (1)
19 Berberis thunbergii atropurpurea Nana (3)
20 Actinidia kolomicta (1)
21 Fatsia japonica (1)
22 Hosta sieboldiana glauca (3)
23 Dicentra spectabilis (3)
24 Cotoneaster dammeri Skogsholm (1)
25 Euphorbia grifithii Fireglow (2)
26 Hebe pinguifolia Pagei (4)
27 Eucalyptus gunnii (1)
28 Acanthus spinosus (3)
29 Cistus silver pink (3)
30 Wisteria sinensis (1)
31 Weigela florida variegata (1)
32 Lilium regale (3)
33 Kerria japonica (2)

Planting plan for a small garden

KEY
1 Cornus alba Elegantissima (2)
2 Arundinaria japonica (3)
3 Potentilla fruticosa Katherine Dykes (2)
4 Spirea bumalda Anthony Waterer (3)
5 Skimmia rubella (2)
6 Cytisus all gold (1)
7 Lupin Russell Hybrids (3)
8 Hydrangea paniculata Grandiflora (2)
9 Hedera colchica (1)
10 Arundinara nitida (1)
11 Bergenia cordifolia (8)
12 Festuca glauca (5)
13 Hibiscus syriacus Woodbridge (1)
14 Lonicera japonica aureo reticulata (1)
15 Cistus cyprius (2)
16 Spirea arguta (2)
17 Lavatera olbia rosea (1)
18 Buddleia davidii empire blue (2)
19 Deutzia scabra Plena (2)
20 Aucuba japonica Variegata (1)
21 Geranium Johnsons Blue (7)
22 Sarcococca humilis (2)
23 Pachysandra terminalis (6)
24 Hydrangea macrophylla blue wave (1)
25 Vinca minor variegata (6)
26 Salvia officinalis purpurascens (2)
27 Festuca scoparius (4)
28 Hebe pinguifolia pagei (2)
29 Lavendula Vera (1)
30 Spirea japonica goldflame (2)
31 Cotoneaster microphyllus (1)
32 Cytisus kewensis (2)

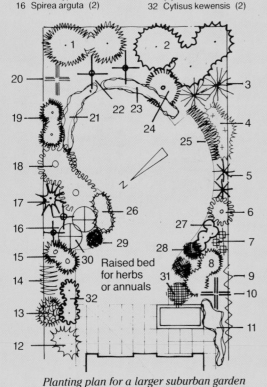

Planting plan for a larger suburban garden

Even shrubs look best if massed together – here brilliant azaleas front a compact pine.

are used singly rather than in drifts or groups. The former approach tends to produce an over-complicated appearance, and the eye is rarely at rest, jumping from one species to the next. Obviously you can include a greater range of species if you choose to use single plants, but this is rarely harmonious in visual terms and you will have a higher level of maintenance, owing to the different cultural requirements of all the plants involved. A rather better approach is to use drifts of material; in a small garden this could mean two or three shrubs of a kind, in a larger garden perhaps five or six. Such drifts could reinforce an underlying design shape, softening a hard corner or leading the eye along a flowing curve.

You can learn a lot from natural growing patterns: in say an oak wood, trees at the highest level give way to a sub-storey of shrubs, which in turn are underplanted with a variety of ground covers such as ivy or honeysuckle. This same strategy can be produced in your own garden and such an approach will do much to reduce maintenance and produce a restful pattern.

We have already seen that the 'hard landscape' provides the framework for our garden, and when working out the planting design we can start with a similar framework of tough, largely evergreen shrubs that will provide shelter, screening and a backdrop to the lighter, more colourful material that can be worked out a little later on.

Understanding plant names

Most people find Latin names complicated; it *is* a specialised language used by horticulturalists and others who deal with plants. Common names can be even more confusing, however, because they can vary wildly from one part of the country to another. When it comes down to it, the Latin ones are not so difficult: most people will recognise 'greyii' as meaning grey, 'purpurea' as purple, 'aurea' as golden and 'hispanica' as coming from Spain for example.

Plants, like animals, are classified into groups and then various 'sub-groups', in a descending hierarchy. You only need to worry about a few of these, but if you can learn to recognise them you will feel much more at home with reading about and buying plants by their Latin names. Without going into the intricacies of botanical classification just look at this: *Berberis thun-bergii atropurpurea* 'Nana'. Quite a mouthful, and it probably sounds like gibberish to many of us. Now, *Berberis* is the *genus*, and if you go into a garden centre and ask for a *Berberis* you can get anything from a tall variety right down to a dwarf plant. All the plants will have certain features in common but the characteristics can still be significantly different. So we need to narrow things down a bit; *thunbergii* is the *species* of the plant and in this case is named after a Mr Thunberg, who was a great plant collector.

The species is always written with a small initial letter, whereas the genus has a capital initial letter, and both are usually italicised. Now you are getting closer, but you might want to narrow it down again. The word *atropurpurea* is the chosen *variety* of the plant, in this case the one with purple leaves; the variety again has a small initial. Finally we come to the *cultivar*.

Cultivars are varieties that do not occur naturally but are the result of intervention by a breeder. The cultivar name always appears within single quotation marks. In this case it is 'Nana', which simply means 'small'. So when it is all broken down we have a 'small, purple-leaved berberis, named after Mr Thunberg'; not so difficult was it? and most impressive at parties!

Plant names are not difficult to learn. Get some good books, visit gardens which are open to the public and where you can see plants labelled, take notes of anything you like and check what conditions they grow in. Remember that other gardeners are friendly people, able and willing to impart free knowledge. One word of advice, however, on selecting plants from books. The size and spread stated will be only an approximate guide, because local conditions may modify these considerably. A shrub planted in a sheltered spot may grow larger than stated; one in an exposed position, rather smaller.

The framework

We have already considered the parameters set by the type of soil, shade and prevailing micro-climatic conditions. Some of the tough, background, evergreen shrubs you are looking for might include *Viburnum rhytidophyllum* with its handsome veined leaves; *Eleagnus ebbingii; Arundinaria nitida*, a graceful bamboo that forms dense clumps; *Viburnum tinus*, with fragrant winter blossom; *Prunus laurocerasus*; ilex (holly); and any number of rhododendrons are just a few. Many of these are 'architectural' in their outline, relying more on the shape and size of foliage for their effect than on a rash of garish colour. In many ways this is just what you want, a strong, quiet background to give you shelter and privacy.

Of course not all background planting need be evergreen, and there are many deciduous shrubs that are an excellent choice. Among these you might think of using forsythia, *Kerria japonica*, philadelphus, weigela and berberis, all having a dense framework of branches that will filter wind and break the line of a bad view even in winter.

Trees

You will have worked out the positions of these in your main layout plan, prepared earlier (page 30) and they will, of course, play an important role in the garden, by screening or framing a view, providing vertical emphasis and casting shadow patterns. Do remember, however, that trees not only come in all shapes and sizes but also have vastly different rates of growth. The all-too-common practice of planting a weeping willow in a small front garden is sheer folly; it may look fine for a couple of years but after that will quickly swamp both the garden and the house it adjoins. There is nothing worse than

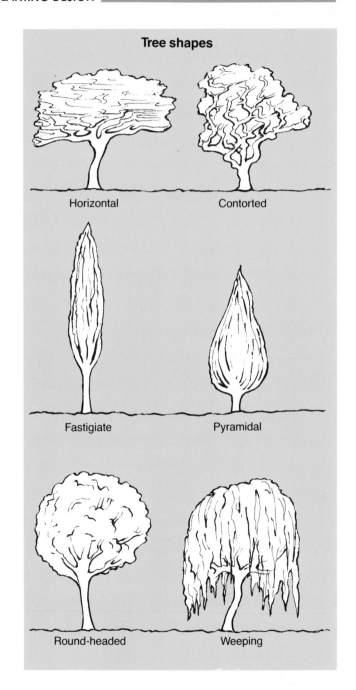

Tree shapes

Horizontal

Contorted

Fastigiate

Pyramidal

Round-headed

Weeping

hacking back such a fine tree that should have been planted in an open position, perhaps by water, with ample room to flourish.

Another reason for not planting such a fast-growing species of tree close to a house is the fact that they extract large quantities of water from the ground, and this can lead to serious damage to foundations. As a guideline, always leave a distance between tree and house equal to the tree's eventual height.

Trees, like shrubs, have different habits or growing patterns. They can be 'horizontal', 'contorted', 'pyramidal', 'round-headed', 'weeping' or 'fastigiate' (conical or tapering). Within these classifications, the size will vary with the species chosen. Fastigiate trees, which have a narrow columnar outline, range from the tall Lombardy poplars or high conifers, which are generally not suitable in a domestic situation, down to the much smaller garden cherry, *Prunus amanagowa*. At the lowest level, miniature conifers reflect the theme. All these fastigiate shapes tend to draw the eye and should be positioned carefully as a 'punctuation mark' to the overall design.

Most of our indigenous trees have a broadly circular or oval growing pattern and these often look most comfortable in our temperate climate. Some ideal species for small gardens might include sorbus (mountain ash and whitebeam), malus (flowering crab apple), betula (birch), many of the prunus (flowering cherries) and for milder parts, eucalyptus (gum). Of course not all trees are simply decorative; fruit trees will give you a supply of apples, pears, cherries and so on. You will also have the benefit of their blossom early in the year. For a small garden there are 'dwarfing' root stocks that keep fruit trees within reasonable proportions, while the new compact, fastigiate fruit trees undoubtedly save a great deal of space and can be grown in the smallest backyard.

Planting trees

While most people take considerable care in preparing the ground for shrubs, trees tend to get a rough deal; they are often dropped into a minimal hole with little support. Always prepare a hole of ample size, allowing at least 30 cm (1 foot) around either the container or around the spread of roots, if the tree is purchased in winter without benefit of a container. Fork the bottom of the hole over and drive a stake firmly into the ground. The stake should be from stout 5 x 5 cm (2 x 2 inch) timber. Position the tree, using the old soil mark around the stem, and backfill around the roots with a planting mixture made up from one part of topsoil, one part of moist peat and three handfuls of bone meal per barrow load. Firm this down as you work. Finally secure the tree to the stake with two plastic or rubber ties, one near the top and one about 45 cm (18 inches) from ground level. Never skimp tree planting: a job well done will repay you in terms of quick establishment and healthy growth. Also, never use a bamboo cane as a support; and don't use a pair of tights, or even worse, wire, to secure the tree. What a shame to pay all that money and yet have a piece of wire cut into the tender stem and have the tree severed in a high wind!

Hedges

Hedges are really an intermediate step between trees and shrubs, and can form boundaries or screens within the boundaries. They are ideal for providing shelter from wind, because they filter rather than create turbulence and are much cheaper than either fences or walls. There are of course disadvantages, in that they take some time to establish and they involve a degree of maintenance. For this reason it makes sense to avoid the rampant hedging species, such as privet and the faster-growing conifers, which can quickly dominate a small garden. Beech, hornbeam and yew are all excellent choices and are not so slow as is often made out, particularly if planted with care in a soil mixture similar to that used for trees. Yew is evergreen, but does have poisonous berries, while beech and hornbeam retain their dead, brown leaves throughout the winter. As far as maintenance is concerned they will need a trim once a year, in late summer, and they can be trained to virtually any height.

The stages of planting a tree

Plant a stake firmly.

Backfill with planting mixture.

Firm down as you work.

Secure the tree safely.

Planting a hedge

Low hedges delineate the beds in this charming traditional rose garden.

Nor need a hedge be a single species. Both plain green and copper beech make an attractive combination, as does holly mixed with yew.

The above are ideal as a formally clipped hedge but there are many species that can be allowed to grow into their natural shape to create an informal pattern. *Rosa rugosa* has long been used in this way, but *Choisya ternata*, escallonia, *Potentilla fruticosa* 'Katherine Dykes', laurel, berberis and many others produce a loose screen.

In design terms, you can move from the formal structure of a clipped hedge to the informality of the unclipped type. This can reflect the theme in a particular part of the garden; formality looks better close to a building.

While all these hedges may be allowed to grow to virtually any height, you can also create a framework at a much lower level. Formal 'parterre' gardens have a long history and can today frame a collection of herbs or perhaps roses. Box *(Buxus suffruticosa)* or lavender are ideal in this context, and can look delightful anywhere in the garden.

Foxgloves and irises fill in gaps between shrubs and other 'framework' plants like roses.

Filling in the pattern

Hedges, trees and the larger 'framework' shrubs will now have provided the framework or back-bone of your planting plan, and it is now time to think about the exciting job of filling in the detail with more colourful smaller shrubs and hardy perennials. Ground-covering plants will also be useful here, as will bulbs and annuals. You now know that plants have all kinds of characteristics, from their shape and size down to their leaf texture and, of course, leaf and flower colour. Before you decide which plants will best fill in the framework you have devised, refer back to pages 82–91 to remind yourself how to use these.

Shrubs and hardy perennials

While shrubs have woody stems that do not die down in winter, the majority of herbaceous plants, or hardy perennials as they are often called, are the opposite, displaying soft stems that do die, although the roots of the plant stay alive to produce new growth next spring.

Unfortunately, the true herbaceous border has largely disappeared from British gardens, but this is a small wonder, because the routine jobs of digging, weeding, feeding, staking, tying and dividing are extremely time-consuming. It is also fair to say that a true herbaceous border, although glorious during the summer months, is dead as a doornail during the winter. If you do want to indulge in this form of planting it is well to site the border in a position that is not normally visible when the plants have died down.

A rather better solution is to build up a border of mixed shrubs and hardy perennials; the shrubs tend to give the perennials support and the latter will provide that necessary colour and interest, and prevent the overall composition from becoming too 'heavy'.

Planting shrubs and hardy perennials

The technique of planting shrubs and hardy perennials is broadly similar to tree planting, but on a smaller scale. Cultivate the ground thoroughly and incorporate as much organic material as possible. Always dig a generous planting hole and use the old soil mark around the stem of the plant as a guide to the new planting depth. Ensure the hole is deep enough and wide enough to allow plenty of planting mixture, made up as for tree planting (page 93), to surround the bare roots or container-grown root-ball. When using container-grown plants, be sure to remove the container carefully so as not to disturb the roots. Remember that a new plant will take a little time to adjust to its new environment, and care, particularly ample irrigation during dry weather, is vital.

Ground-covering plants

Although we have already discussed the usefulness of these particular plants when used as a single element to reduce maintenance, they also have a rôle in the mixed border. Here they can also be used in drifts, but as under-planting to the taller shrubs and herbaceous plants. In this setting they will certainly reduce weed-growth by blanketing the ground, but care should be taken to see that they do not invade neighbouring plants. If a particular ground cover becomes too invasive, it should be cut back or a section dug out altogether.

Apart from their advantage as weed suppressors, they can be used as a drift beneath several groups of shrubs and will provide natural continuity in this way.

Ground-covering plants are essentially small shrubs, and the technique for planting them is much the same. The illustration on page 94 explain the stages.

Ground covering plants such as heathers can reduce maintenance to a minimum.

Bulbs

Although there are bulbs that flower throughout the year, most people tend to think of bulbs as the heralds of spring. There are really two ways to plant them, either in straight lines, which inevitably tends to look rather 'municipal', or in a more informal setting, perhaps under trees, set in slightly longer grass in an informal part of the garden.

If you like the regimented approach then it is best implemented close to the house, where the strong patterns created will tend to echo the equally strong lines of the architecture. It is also sensible to keep to a single colour in this sort of situation; if a composition is going to be positive then make it really positive! Such a display is usually lifted after the bulbs have died down and is replaced by annual bedding plants. The bulbs can be allowed to dry off and can then be stored in a cool and shady place for use the following year.

The informal approach involves naturalising the bulbs, in other words you leave them in position and simply let them die down in the spring to reappear next season. This being the case the grass should not be cut until the leaves of the bulbs have gone brown, indicating that all the goodness has returned to the bulb itself.

As well as planting bulbs informally in a rough grass area, perhaps with wild flowers, you could introduce them into the general borders, where they will make a welcome splash of colour early

Spring bulbs are at their best in an informal, grassy area.

in the year. If you adopt this approach, it's worth making a garden plan of where you have put the bulbs, to help you avoid digging them up later! If you do dig up a bulb by mistake, replant it at the same depth.

Annual bedding plants
It is best to use annual bedding plants (hardy and half-hardy annuals and hardy biennials) in a broadly similar way to bulbs: an architectural approach close to the house or drifts of colour in the general borders. Using such plants is quite labour-intensive, because they need to be planted out each spring, after the frosts, and to be removed at the end of the season, when they are killed by the first hard weather of the autumn. You can either buy bedding plants in boxes, already grown for you, or sow them yourself in a greenhouse, prick out the tiny plants and then grow them on yourself, away from the frost, ready to plant out at around the middle of May.

Some annuals are dramatic plants, take sunflowers for instance. Others are fragrant, such as night-scented stocks or nicotiana. All can have their place, but, as with all kinds of planting, do your homework first, check the eventual size and colour and then plan accordingly.

A winter garden of heathers and conifers provides interest during the cold months.

PRACTICALITIES

In this day of the well stocked garden centre that offers a wide range of shrubs, conifers and hardy perennials of different sizes, it could be said that there is little need to know how plants grow. In many ways this is true, for if you follow the guidelines set out on the plant labels and have a background knowledge of the basic cultivation and after-care techniques, your plants should develop without any problems. Buying well grown material in this way can be reasonably expensive, however, particularly if you have large areas to cover, and there are other, far more cost-effective ways that you can employ to get new plants started. It is also true to say that if you understand how plants grow, you will see reasons for the need to prune and feed, and why pests and diseases can become a problem in the garden.

There are a number of different ways of getting plants to grow and the general term for this is 'propagation'. The method employed depends on the type of plant, but the most common techniques include growing from seed, taking cuttings, division and layering. There are other methods, such as budding and grafting, but these are rather more specialised and have less chance of success for the novice gardener.

Growing from seed

There is no 'right' or 'wrong' way of propagation, but some techniques favour particular kinds of plants. Sowing seed is a cheap and convenient way of producing large numbers of small plants. It is by far the best way of reproducing half-hardy annuals, hardy annuals and biennials. It is not so suitable for many herbaceous varieties, because the new plants will rarely breed 'true' from seed: the resulting plants may be different from the parents in colour, or may be inferior. Neither is it a satisfactory way of propagating shrubs, because, again the plants may not be true to type. It also takes many years to grow most shrubs from seed, and it can be difficult to persuade the seeds to 'germinate' (start growing).

Part of the fun of growing from seed is in poring over catalogues or browsing through the displays of packets at your local garden centre. It is also true to say that actually seeing a tiny, seemingly dead grain of material grow into a glorious, flower-laden plant is sheer magic. Children in particular are enthralled, and this in itself can be the best of reasons for growing from seed; not only to start a young gardener on a lifetime's hobby, but simply to bring you the pleasure of their enjoyment.

Half-hardy annuals
Half-hardy annuals form the major part of bedding displays during the summer. The term 'half-hardy' means that they must be protected from cold while the plants are young. They are raised in the spring, indoors or in a greenhouse; are transplanted into the garden after the last frosts, usually towards the end of May; and they die in

the first frosts of autumn. They include such favourites as ageratum, antirrhinum, (snapdragons), bedding begonias, calceolarias, bedding dahlias, impatiens (busy lizzie), lobelias, petunias, and salvias. There are many more, as the seed catalogues amply testify.

Seed should be bought ready for sowing during March and April and should be planted in a peat-based seed compost in seed trays or pots. Ensure the container or pot has drainage holes to prevent waterlogging. Fill the container with compost, firm the surface down with a piece of board, and dampen the compost the evening before sowing. Sow the seed thinly but as evenly as possible and scatter a thin layer of compost on top, again firming the surface down. Always insert a label; it is more than frustrating, when growing a number of different species, if you forget just what is in which box!

There are two easy methods of persuading the seeds to germinate. The first is to moisten the compost, place a piece of glass over the container and cover this with newspaper. Keep it warm: an ideal temperature is 18–21°C (65–70°F). When the seedlings appear, remove the paper and prop the glass up all round to provide ventilation. Keep the compost moist, it should be damp not dry, but not obviously wet. Ensure the young plants are kept in a light position. It is very important not to over-water at this stage.

Once the leaves have expanded you can carefully remove small clumps of plants, divide them, and plant the individual seedlings in other pots or trays, also filled with potting compost. The plants should be spaced about 5 cm (2 inches) apart. This process is known as 'pricking out'. Gently firm them in and moisten the compost. The young plants should then be kept in a shady position for a few days.

Once the plants have picked up they can start

Newspaper

Glass

Prop up the glass to allow ventilation.

The correct stage for 'pricking out'.

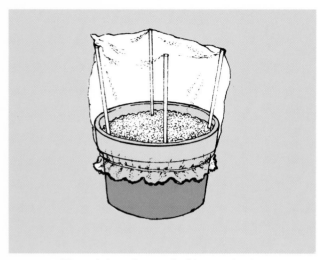

The polythene bag method for germination

to be 'hardened off', that is, gradually accustomed to being outside, ready for transplanting to their final position. If you have a cold frame they can be moved into this; gradually increase the ventilation and finally remove the cover completely. If you do not have a frame, move the boxes outside during the day and bring them in at night. Once all chance of frost is over plant them out. It is easy to construct a simple cold frame.

An even simpler way of growing half-hardy annuals is to sow seed in a pot of seed compost, moisten the compost, and cover the pot with a transparent polythene bag secured with a rubber band. As soon as the seedlings break through, remove the bag and place the pot on a windowsill, turning regularly so that the plants develop evenly.

The best time for planting is during late May and early June, once the frosts are finished. Water the plants a couple of hours before you use them, and make sure the ground is well prepared and broken down into a fine tilth. Using a trowel, dig a hole that will be large enough to accept the depth and spread of the roots; the top of the compost around the new plant should be marginally below soil level when planted. Remove a plant from the tray or pot and plant it immediately. Never leave young plants lying on the ground waiting to be planted; they dry out very quickly. Replace the soil around the plant, firm it in gently with your fingers and water it.

Although ordinary garden soil can be used for filling in around newly planted annuals you will give them an even better start if you prepare a special planting mixture. This can be made up from one part moist peat, one part topsoil and three handfuls of bone meal per barrow load.

Hardy annuals
These plants also grow and flower in a single season, but, unlike half-hardy annuals, they can be planted straight into the ground either during March and April or in the September previous to flowering. If doing the former, ensure the ground is dry enough for thorough cultivation to prepare a seed bed, and warm enough to encourage germination. Don't sow if the weather is cold and wet, therefore. Plants can 'catch up' if they are put in a bit late.

Examples of hardy annuals are alyssum, anchusa, calendula, (marigold), clarkia, godetia, iberis, lathyrus (sweet pea), nigella and schizanthus.

Thorough preparation of the seed bed, ensuring a fine tilth, is essential, and it is possible just to scatter the seed over the areas you wish to cover. However, the failure of some seeds to germinate could create an uneven growth pattern and lead to problems in weeding and thinning out later. It is better to mark the bed out and sow seed directly and thinly into shallow grooves or 'drills'. These should be watered *before* planting and not after, because it is all too easy to wash seeds away.

Sow the seed thickly and cover it with a depth of soil roughly twice the diameter of the seeds themselves. Protect from birds by criss-crossing the drills with twigs or black cotton. Seedlings appear with two sets of leaves: the first are simple and rounded; the second set are more developed and show the characteristics of the mature

plant. Once these second leaves have developed, thin the row very carefully to a plant every 5 cm (2 inches). Between one and two weeks later thin the plants again to their final spacing, which will be between 15 and 30 cm (6–12 inches) apart, depending on the type and eventual size of the plant. Be careful not to disturb the roots of the remaining plants you are thinning. Seed sown in September should be thinned out in the autumn, once the seedlings have developed.

Hardy biennials
Hardy biennials can also be grown from seed and are very useful for filling in the gaps between shrubs and hardy perennials while these are developing. They are sown outside in the summer, produce stems and leaves in the first season, over-winter, and then flower and die in the coming year. Examples are bellis, campanula, cheiranthus (wallflower), digitalis (foxglove), lunaria (honesty), myosotis and viola (pansy).

The best way of growing them is to have a separate bed in which the seed can be germinated and the young plants can be allowed to develop before being planted out in their final positions. This bed should be well prepared and the seed sown in drills spaced 30 cm (1 foot) apart, during early summer. Remember to label the rows carefully. Thin the plants out as for half-hardy and hardy annuals, leaving a gap of about 5 cm (2 inches) between plants. These should be firmed in.

During October, carefully lift the plants with a trowel, keeping soil around the roots, and position them in their final places in the border. Water the plants gently if the weather is dry.

Growing from cuttings

While most annuals are best grown from seed, and most herbaceous or hardy perennials benefit

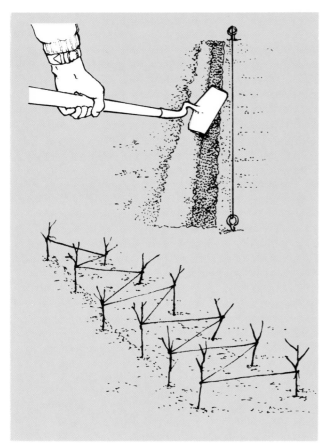

Marking seed drills (above) and protecting the seed bed when sown (below).

Taking geranium cuttings: an easy and satisfying method of home propagation.

Shrubs

Most shrubs are best propagated by taking cuttings either in July and August or in November. Buddleia, ceonothus, cotoneaster, escallonia, pieris, potentilla, spirea and viburnum are good examples of shrubs that are best propagated in summer under glass; either 'stem tip' cuttings or 'heel' cuttings are the best methods.

The wood should be starting to ripen, and healthy side shoots that are still soft at the top but woodier further down are ideal for cuttings. The length of the cutting will depend on the type of shrub and for both heel and stem cuttings the leaves should be removed from the bottom half of the shoot.

For stem cuttings, select a leaf joint near the bottom and make a straight cut to remove it from the wood below. Dip the stem into a rooting hormone and place the cuttings in a 15 cm (6-inch) pot that is filled with seed-and-cutting compost; you can usually fit several cuttings into one pot. If the leaves are broad, such as rhododendron or laurel, then you can trim them in half. Water sparingly.

Heel cuttings should be treated in exactly the same way as above, except that the 'heel' is left intact. You can use either technique on most shrubs; neither has particular advantages over the other.

Place summer cuttings in a cold frame, which should have ample ventilation in hot weather; alternatively cover the pot with a polythene bag, supported on canes sunk in the pot. If using the latter method, place the pot in ample light but away from direct sun. Any leaves that die off should be removed, and in spring the rooted plants should be placed in a 'nurse' bed, prior to final planting out in the autumn.

Autumn cuttings do not need the protection of glass and they can be planted directly outside in

from division, many shrubs are best propagated from cuttings. There are of course exceptions to any rule and both pelargoniums (geraniums) and fuchsias are also excellent material for cuttings.

Geraniums are easy to root and you should select the ends of non-flowering shoots about 10 cm (4 inches) long, during July and August, planting these in seed-and-cutting compost. Don't cover the cuttings and there is no need to use a hormone rooting powder. They should root in about three weeks, after which they can be transferred to pots filled with potting compost. Cuttings should be over-wintered either in a cold greenhouse or in an unheated room, and while water can be given sparingly there is no need to feed the young plants.

Fuchsia cuttings can be taken either in spring or summer, again using non-flowering shoots about 7 cm (3 inches) long and a seed-and-cutting compost. Rooting should take place in three weeks and the plants can then be transplanted into 7 cm (3-inch) pots filled with potting compost.

Taking a stem cutting

Select a suitable shoot.

Remove leaves below the second set.

For 'stem' cuttings, make a straight cut.

For 'heel' cuttings, cut away the heel of the shoot too.

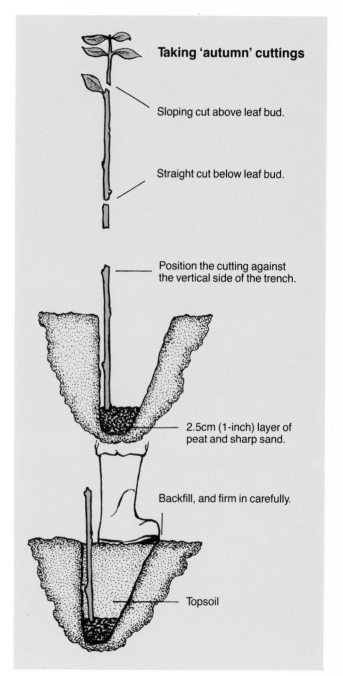

Taking 'autumn' cuttings

Sloping cut above leaf bud.

Straight cut below leaf bud.

Position the cutting against the vertical side of the trench.

2.5cm (1-inch) layer of peat and sharp sand.

Backfill, and firm in carefully.

Topsoil

November. Shrubs suitable for this technique include aucuba, cornus, deutzia, lonicera (honeysuckle), kerria, philadelphus, ribes, *Sambucus symphoricarpus* and weigela.

Once again, select a healthy stem, about 30 cm (12 inches) long. Remove the top of the stem with a sloping cut above a leaf bud, and the bottom below a bud with a straight cut. Prepare a trench approximately 15 cm (6 inches) deep, with one vertical and one sloping side. Place the cuttings 15 cm (6 inches) apart in the trench, against the vertical side, with a third above ground level. Place a 2.5 cm (1-inch) layer of peat and sharp (gritty) sand in the bottom and then replace the topsoil, firming this in carefully as you progress. Water well and also firm the cuttings back in if frost disturbs the ground during winter. Water throughout the next summer. The rooted cuttings should be ready for planting out in their final positions in the autumn.

Layering

Some shrubs that have long, drooping stems can be easily propagated by the technique known as

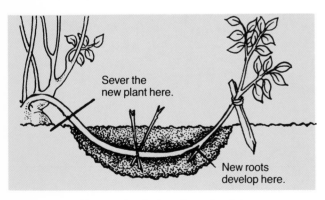

Sever the
new plant here.

New roots
develop here.

Propagation by layering: when it is established, sever the new plant from the parent.

'layering', and in fact this happens quite naturally in species like honeysuckle or rhododendron.

Select a young shoot and peg the middle of it down in a hole about 15 cm (6 inches) deep with twigs; fill the hole with a mixture of good topsoil and peat. If you like, make a slit in the stem before planting and insert a sliver of wood to hold it open. It will be at this point that the new roots develop and making a slit encourages this to happen more quickly. Where the stem re-appears above ground, neatly stake the end as shown in the illustration. Rooting will take place in a year or less and the new plant can then be severed from the parent and planted out in its new position.

Division

Division is by far the best method of increasing hardy perennials or herbaceous plants. In fact, dividing these types of plants is essential to keep them healthy, because after about three years the centre of the perennial becomes woody and largely unproductive, the healthy, vigorous growth being concentrated around the perimeter. Both spring and autumn are ideal times for division of most varieties but make sure the ground is not waterlogged.

Dig up the whole clump and shake off excess soil. Many plants are too tough to divide by hand and are best prised into sections with two garden forks, positioned back to back. Cut away the inferior centre sections and replant the healthy stock in its new position. Most herbaceous plants will divide into three or four parts. Water in well after planting and re-label if you wish.

Some plants, such as iris, sprout from 'rhizomes', which are thick underground stems. These stems have fibrous roots and the whole clump can be lifted and divided with a sharp knife, usually in summer. The divisions should have healthy growth above and ample root below the rhizome. Discard any dead or diseased sections and re-plant at a similar depth.

Bulbs, if naturalised to form drifts and clumps in the garden also benefit from being lifted every few years. Once they have died down after flowering, lever them up with a fork and carefully prise them apart by hand. The larger bulbs will flower the following season after replanting but you will also have plenty of 'bulblets' which will take two or three years to produce flowers. These can be replanted in the borders immediately, but are easily disturbed by cultivation, so you might prefer to plant them in a special area, out of the way, and re-position them once they do eventually flower.

Protecting plants

Having gone to the trouble and expense of growing or buying your plants, it would be foolish to offer them no protection against the elements!

Wind
Wind will be the major problem and for the larger elements in the garden, namely trees, adequate staking is a necessity. We have already seen how this should be on page 93.

Shrubs are self-supporting on the whole, provided that they are planted at the right depth and firmed in well. By the time they grow to their full height, the root system will be well developed and able to provide ample anchorage.

Herbaceous and hardy perennials are slightly different, however, as the majority of these grow new foliage from ground level each spring. Some species, such as the taller varieties of delphinium or chrysanthemum, will benefit from support. Push bamboo canes well into the ground and fasten the plants to these with soft garden twine.

Tall plants may need to be supported by canes.

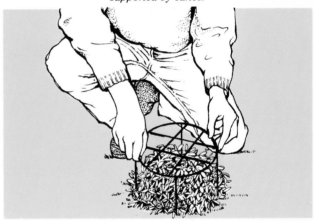

A wire frame can support a bushier, lower-growing plant.

Bushier types of plant such as cimicifuga and gypsophila can be supported by wire frames that can be purchased from your garden centre. Position these over the plants in the spring and the stems will grow through and be gently held in position.

Another problem with wind is that it can dry out the foliage of certain plants, particularly when they are vulnerable after transplanting;

conifers are particularly susceptible to this. You can use an anti-desiccant spray to help seal the leaf pores through which the plant transpires. On a windy site it can also be helpful to position a temporary wind break on the windward side of such plants. A suitable wind break can be made from stout posts driven into the ground so that the tops are just higher than the plants themselves. Nail hessian or fine plastic mesh to the posts to break the force of the wind. The first season's growth should be enough for the plant to stabilise and settle into its new position.

Frost
Some plants are less hardy, and thus more susceptible to very low temperatures, than others. Species such as agapanthus, schizostylis and gunnera could be killed by a severe winter if left unprotected. The best way to protect them is to cover the plants, once they have died down in the autumn, with wire netting covered with straw. Use another piece of netting, pegged down, to complete the cover. The leaves of gunnera, which are particularly large, can be cut down and laid over the plant as protection.

Snow
While snow is a great insulator of plant material, it can have an altogether different effect on evergreen plants, and conifers in particular. A heavy fall will collect on branches and leaves, forcing the stems outwards and even breaking them altogether. Shrubs can usually be shaken to remove snow, and this applies to conifers too. However, the latter may benefit from being tied up to hold the branches together; shake the tree, or knock the snow off, after any accumulation.

Damp
Alpine plants are remarkably hardy and some are able to withstand witheringly low temperatures. This is aided in their natural habitat by an insulating cover of snow. In our climate, however, snow is often replaced by cold, wet weather, and this can rot those tiny stems and roots. The best protection here is to cover them during winter with a plastic or glass cloche, ensuring that there is plenty of ventilation.

Moving plants

In even the best-planned garden, there may well come a time when you need to move trees, shrubs and herbaceous plants. This can become necessary when a border has been thickly planted to achieve rapid maturity and some plants need thinning out. It can also be a useful technique if screening from a new house or other development is needed. A tree from another part of the garden could be used for this.

Moving trees
The only time to move deciduous trees is during their dormant season. This roughly extends between November and March, when the leaves have fallen. Specimens over about 3.75 m (12 feet) are really too large, as the physical effort to dig and move the large root ball involved is enormous.

The work should be carried out in mild, frost-free weather, when the soil is not waterlogged. Before moving the tree, prepare a new planting hole in the correct position.

The first step is to make a vertical cut with a spade in the ground around the tree, approximately along a line equal to the spread of the branches. To protect the latter during removal and transit, tie them in with strips of hessian, being careful not to do this too tightly and snap the stems. The vertical cut will probably sever a

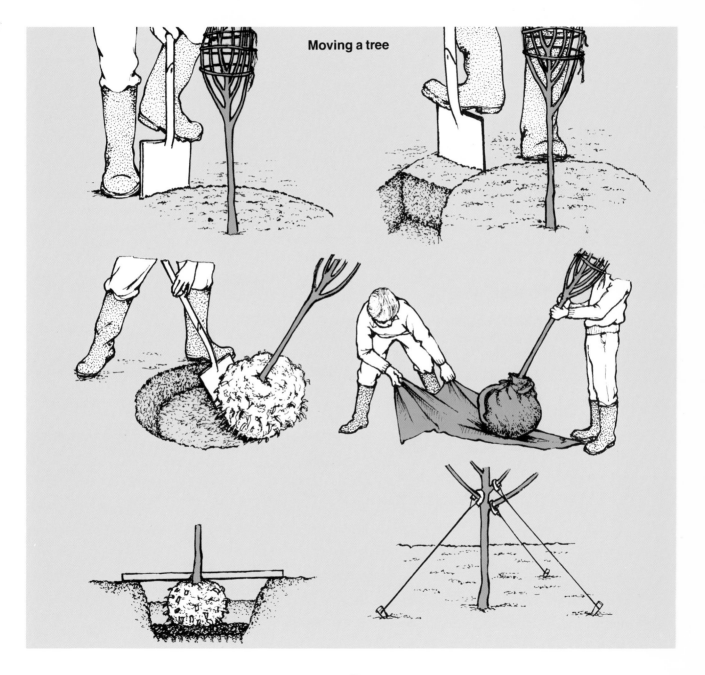

Moving a tree

number of roots, some of which may be pretty tough.

Once the slit is complete, dig around the outside, forming a trench of one spade's depth. The next job is to undercut the root ball, working the spade in at an angle of about 45 degrees. Do this all round and start to ease the tree backwards and forwards, cutting any downward-growing roots. While doing this try to keep as much of the soil around the tree as possible.

When you can rock the root ball completely over, slide a sheet of polythene underneath and wrap this up around the stem, tying it off. If the tree is heavy – and it is amazing how even a quite small specimen and root ball seems almost too heavy to move – get ample help. Ease it out of the hole on to a polythene sack and slide it over to the new position.

Once there, measure the depth of the ball from the old planting height and adjust the depth of the hole accordingly. Fork over the bottom and add compost, manure and two handfuls of bone meal. Position the tree and backfill the hole in layers, firming the soil as you go. It is difficult to support a tree like this with a single stake and it can be better to fit several wire guy lines, sleeved in sections of hose pipe, to branches, and lead these back to pegs securely hammered into the ground.

Large conifers are particularly difficult to move, with a high failure rate, although smaller sizes are more successful. Spray with an anti-desiccant and protect both deciduous and coniferous trees with a screen of hessian nailed to stakes, if necessary. If the weather is dry, a lot of water may be needed, particularly in the spring and summer after the re-planting.

Moving shrubs
The technique of moving shrubs is very much the same as that for moving trees, but on a smaller and less energetic scale. Thorough preparation of the new site is essential. This can also be a good opportunity to remove any dead or diseased wood, pruning the stems to an altogether better shape. If moving plants from a crowded border you may find that this is particularly necessary, because growth could well have become distorted owing to the proximity of neighbours. Staking shrubs after planting is not usually necessary. Deciduous shrubs can be moved between November and March. Evergreen shrubs are best moved in September or October, or in April. Ensure that the ground is not waterlogged or frozen solid.

Feeding plants

The problem with many gardens is the simple fact that people forget to feed their plants, which, like any organism, need nourishment to keep them vigorous and healthy. When you buy plants grown in containers they come in soil that includes a slow-release fertiliser, and this will give them enough nourishment for that vital first season. After that, however, you need to take matters into your own hands.

We looked at the basic differences between organic and inorganic fertilisers on pages 35–6. Any garden will benefit from the introduction of well rotted compost and manure on a regular basis, usually during autumn. Not everyone will have access to this kind of bulky plant food, however, and there are a number of other excellent organic fertilisers available. Many of these come in liquid form and can be simply added to a watering can and applied either by hand or through an automatic watering system. This type of plant food is fast acting and should be applied during the summer months.

Inorganic fertilisers are usually in pellet form and are by their nature slow-release types. They can be sprinkled around the base of plants in spring to encourage growth throughout the summer.

Lawns

Grass is a small plant and needs feeding like everything else in the garden. There are two main times to do this; during the spring and again in the autumn. Combined fertilisers and weed-killers can be used, and these are available in liquid or pellet form. Always check application rates. If using the pellet type, there are wheeled spreaders that make the job very simple indeed.

Trees and hedges

While most of us understand the importance of feeding shrubs, lawns and herbaceous plants, the poor old trees and hedges often get overlooked altogether. Both are plants and take a lot of goodness out of the ground. Hedges can be treated in the same way as shrubs in the general border (page 97); always incorporate a slow-release fertiliser when planting. Trees are slightly different, particularly when they have been established for some while. If they are positioned in a lawn, spike the lawn well in spring with a garden fork all over the area covered by the branches. Brush a slow-release fertiliser into the holes, and, if the weather remains dry, water well after a few days.

Irrigation

Water is essential to all plant life and while we naturally assume that most gardens are open to the elements, and therefore to rain, there can be quite large areas that receive little or no moisture at all. The line of boundary walls or overhanging eaves can form a 'rain shadow', effectively screen-

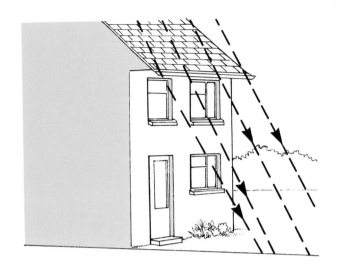

Conditions in a rain shadow make it surprisingly hard for plants to receive enough water.

ing the ground below. Such a shadow can occur in any garden where structures are present. If you carried out your survey thoroughly you should have pinpointed any such positions, and either eliminated planting or realised that it will need watering on a regular basis.

Rain shadows aside, it will be sensible to plan for irrigating the garden in some way. In the most basic form irrigation will involve a garden tap, watering can and length of hose. However, manufacturers have become far more sophisticated than that these days, and there are excellent 'snap-together' hosepipe systems with a multitude of heads and sprays. Some of these are designed to incorporate fertiliser at the same time. Remember that any tap and associated pipework in the garden should be well lagged against winter frost. It is preferable to turn off the water supply at this time of year and drain away surplus water in the pipes back to the stop-cock.

Perforated hoses can be useful laid across a lawn or through a border, while rotary and oscillating sprinklers extend the range of irrigation and can be quickly and easily moved around the garden.

Automatic systems are now becoming increasingly popular and cheaper. These can be bought in kit form and consist of small-bore pipes and spray heads that snap together and can therefore be tailored to your plot. They can be manually operated or worked off a pre-set timer. The most complicated systems of all are fully automated with 'pop-up' heads and usually have to be installed by specialist companies. They can be operated by computer and may incorporate facilities for automatic feeding. Such systems can also overcome the problem of low water pressure, having their own built-in pumps. Whatever system you use, understand its capabilities and remember that in most areas you will need to inform the water authority that you have such a system. Check whether you need a licence for this or any other kind of irrigation system in the garden, including an ordinary hosepipe.

Pests and diseases

It would be beyond the scope of this book to list all the pests and diseases that can attack trees, shrubs and hardy perennials. In truth, if plants are chosen carefully, planted correctly and given adequate food to keep them vigorous, then you should have little difficulty in keeping things in excellent order. From time to time, however, you may need to resort to pest-control preparations.

Problems with plants are broadly caused by attacks by insect pests and by fungal diseases.

Insect pests
Of these, there are two types; firstly, creatures that chew leaves, flowers, fruit or roots, such as caterpillars; the larvae of beetles; woodlice; earwigs; slugs and snails. On a far larger scale, rabbits and occasionally deer can be a real problem. The second kind are insects that suck; aphids are the best known, and these include blackfly and greenfly. Other suckers are whitefly and scale insects. While those that chew leave obvious holes in leaves and fruit, the sucking variety tend to weaken the plant by removing sap.

Pesticides kill these insects, but I must say that I only use such chemicals when an infestation is genuinely bad. Of the chemicals there are those that kill by direct contact with the pest and those that work by being absorbed by the plants and then being ingested by the pest concerned. Aphids are particularly susceptible to this latter form of insecticide, which is called 'systemic', because it enters the system of the plant.

Fungal diseases
Moulds, mildew, rust and black spot are the most common kinds of fungal diseases. The usual treatment is with a group of chemicals known as fungicides. The best types to use are systemic fungicides that penetrate the whole plant system and eradicate disease wherever it resides.

The best way to control disease is by prevention. This means removing all rotten foliage left at the end of a season, and plant prunings, because these are the most common places where disease originates.

Mould and mildew are easily spotted, and if you catch them early it can be sufficient simply to remove the offending leaves and burn them. If the attack is worse, spray immediately with a systemic fungicide. Black spot and rust can be found in roses throughout the summer, the latter being the less common of the two. Both respond to spraying, and fallen leaves should be immediately removed and burnt. Mildew on roses is usually apparent in summer or early autumn, and can also be controlled by spraying.

Using chemicals
Names of chemical insecticides are long and complicated but any good garden centre will have a range of products from different manufacturers that will tackle any of these problems. The directions and particular problem to be tackled will be clearly displayed, but if in any doubt, *always* ask.

For my own part, I am one of those gardeners who avoids using chemicals if at all possible, and it is most welcome that a number of manufacturers and garden centres are offering products with an organic base. These will be clearly packaged, as will ozone-friendly sprays.

It is worth stressing at this point that any weed-killer or pesticide should be kept well out of the reach of children, locked away if possible, and should *never* be stored in any container other than the original packaging. Fatal accidents do happen, and could nearly always have been avoided. There are no shortcuts to safety, so always be careful. Always carry out instructions to the letter and do not use more or a stronger mixture than stated; this will simply do more harm than good.

Trees and shrubs are not generally prone to disease, and attack by aphids or caterpillars can be controlled by spraying when they are first identified. Certain trees are prone to specific diseases; cherries, for instance, often contract peach leaf curl, but again this can easily be controlled by annual spraying early in the year. Other plants attract specified pests: rhododendrons can suffer from a particular insect, while holly is prone to the leaf miner grub. These and

many others can, however, be controlled, although it is fair to say that a few are fatal.

Herbaceous plants are slightly more susceptible to attack, because their soft, fleshy stems are an easier prospect for pests and diseases. The same basic rules of preparation and feeding apply: happy plants are healthy plants! It can be useful to keep a small standby pack of fungicide and insecticide handy. Add to this slug pellets (you can get these in organic form now) and remember that it is better to renew your stock of these preparations each year than to use old and possibly ineffective materials.

If plants are attacked and you take remedial action it is particularly important to apply a liquid feed afterwards, to speed their recovery.

Pruning

The very mention of pruning strikes confusion into the heart of a novice gardener, and this is due in part to the over-complicated way this simple subject is dealt with by professionals.

If you look at trees and shrubs in their natural hedgerow habitat you will see that, although they are vigorous, they are also tangled and unkempt. This is due partly to a lack of available plant food, but rather more to the plant's struggling for light and air, and in so doing growing ever higher.

In the garden, there are three basic reasons for pruning, the first of which is to keep the tree or shrub within reasonable proportions. Obviously if you choose your plant material carefully this need can largely be eliminated, but there is often a desire to grow a particular favourite that may need a little supervision!

The second reason is to maintain health and vigour. This means that those long straggly shoots can be shortened and stems that grow into the centre of a plant can be removed to allow the penetration of light and air. Weak, damaged or diseased wood can be removed at the same time. Pruning will regulate the flowering pattern, and this constitutes the third reason for pruning. The result of pruning is that you are shortening the stems, allowing the buds below the cut to shoot. This will produce healthy, vigorous and well shaped plants.

Different plants are, however, pruned in slightly different ways and at somewhat different times. As a general rule, deciduous shrubs that flower in early spring up to early June should be pruned immediately after they flower. Examples include cytisus, forsythia and ribes. Cut back the flowering shoots and remove any dead or diseased wood. Deciduous shrubs that flower after this time should be pruned between January and March; examples here would include buddleia, hypericum and hydrangea. Evergreen shrubs are best pruned in May, while conifers should be left till autumn.

Some shrubs are grown for the colour of their winter stems: cornus and the smaller varieties of willow are good examples. These should be cut back hard to within two or three buds of the old wood in March. This will give them the whole summer and autumn to produce stems.

Ground-covering plants need to be just that, and to keep them as a neat carpet clip them over with a pair of shears in spring. Species such as *Hypericum calycinum,* vinca and heathers will respond well, and also keep maintenance to a minimum if kept tight to the ground.

Clematis inevitably spread confusion and it is worth outlining the pruning techniques involved. There are three groups; firstly, those that flower early in the year, including the *C. montana* types and species such as *C. macropetala*. These can largely be left alone and they are ideal for covering a large area of wall or unsightly garage. If they do get out of hand, prune them after flowering but not too hard or you will lose the next year's blooms.

Varieties such as the favourite 'Nellie Moser' flower in early summer and these, together with the mid-summer flowerers that include 'Ville de Lyon' and *Clematis × jackmanii* should be pruned earlier; in February, if possible. They can be cut hard back to within 30 cm (12 inches) of the ground, to just above a strong pair of buds.

The last type is late-summer-flowering, *C. tangutica* and *C. viticella* being examples. As these are vigorous they can be cut back to a pair of buds just above ground level, also in February.

Most shrubs are too large to 'deadhead' effectively, but it is worth pinching out rhododendron blooms after flowering, which helps the next year's buds, and neatly removing lilac blooms with secateurs if you can reach them. Annuals and hardy perennials can be deadheaded and this will often encourage repeat flowering.

Roses
Roses are probably the world's favourite plant and hardly a garden is without them. Pruning is not difficult but most people are afraid to carry it out hard enough.

The hybrid tea types should be pruned to within 4–6 buds of the ground to a bud that faces the garden not the centre of the rose. This prevents stems from growing into the centre of the plant, and keeps the shape well balanced and open. Floribundas should be pruned slightly less hard, but in the same way, to 6–8 buds from the ground. March is the ideal month for carrying out pruning and don't be tricked into doing it earlier by an unseasonal warm spell.

Climbing and rambling roses only need light pruning if they become overgrown. Dead wood and weaker shoots can be removed in the spring. Removing spent blooms or 'deadheading' all types of roses is an important summer job, and helps maintain the production of flowers.

PROJECTS

The problem with many gardens is that they are tackled back to front. By this I mean that features and furnishings are assembled before the main framework of the design has been worked out. We have already seen that this usually spells visual disaster, and that it is essential to plan the garden as an overall concept, into which a number of incidental projects can be fitted later on.

In fact, the success of a well-thought-out composition is that it is open to modification and change, particularly as a family develops and grows older. In this way the garden becomes infinitely extendable, and new features can be added, others modified or subtracted as time goes by. Another advantage of the 'extendable' approach is the simple fact that you can spread the cost over a period of time. This means that a built-in barbecue, rockery and waterfall, play area or pergola, all of which involve a reasonable outlay in effort and cash, can be planned from the beginning and added when you wish.

Some projects are a major undertaking, others are virtually instant. Whatever they are they should be tackled with good design sense, and, perhaps most importantly, safety in mind.

Window boxes

Window-boxes are tiny gardens in their own right and can be equally delightful in the heart of a city, where space is at a premium, or outside a country house set in rolling acres.

Such containers can be filled with the half-hardy annual plants that we discussed earlier (page 99), or with a more permanent display of small shrubs and ground-covering plants that can provide interest throughout the year. Wooden boxes are traditionally used and these can be easily constructed to fit the required opening exactly, although there are plenty of plastic and terracotta troughs available, which eliminate carpentry altogether. If choosing plastic, remember that the beauty of the material lies in its strength and its ability to be moulded into

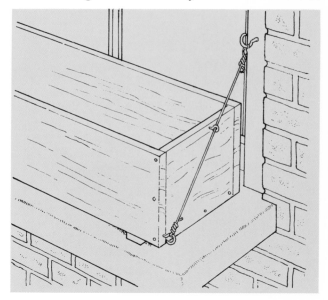

sensible shapes. There will be an opportunity for the container to pick up a colour inside the house, reinforcing the link between home and garden. Try to avoid plastic that imitates another material such as timber or lead; the fake is usually obvious and the end result visually dishonest.

Whatever the material, window-boxes should be approximately 22 cm (9 inches) deep and the same wide. This will allow ample root development, and hold sufficient soil to minimise drying out.

If the boxes are made from timber, adequate protection from weather is vital. You should either paint the wood with primer, undercoat and exterior gloss, or apply two coats of a non-toxic preservative. Drainage holes should be incorporated in the bottom. Feet will lift the box above the sill, to prevent the timber rotting, and, if the sill slopes the feet can be shaped so that the container is horizontal. Use brass screws for fixing. For added safety, fit screw eyes to the bottom front of the box and thread some wire back through a second set of eyes fixed to the top of the box at the back; finally secure the wires to the window-frame by tying them on to hooks. This is absolutely vital if the containers are set in a position from where they might fall on someone below.

When filling the window-box, first place a layer of broken earthenware 'crocks' over the bottom to help drainage. For permanent planting, half-fill the box with John Innes No. 2 potting compost. Position the plants, adding more compost as the plants are firmed into position. A good collection might include miniature conifers and heathers while ivy, *Euonymus* 'Silver Queen', *Hebe pinguifolia pagei* or santolina are just a few shrubs that will provide year-round colour. Herbs would also be an ideal choice, particularly on a kitchen window sill.

Annual plants can be treated in the same way and in the same compost, although an alternative is to keep the plants in their pots, and surround these with peat. However plants used in this way will dry out far more quickly and will need more frequent watering. Feeding will also be important; give a liquid fertiliser once every two weeks. Suitable annuals include many of the 'bedding' varieties including tagetes, ageratum, petunias, ivy-leafed perlargoniums, busy lizzie, verbena and trailing lobelia. Be sure to remove spent blooms regularly and when the summer display is over, plant bulbs for a spring display. Water window-boxes once a day in the evening. In very hot weather, water morning *and* evening, but not when the box is in full sun.

A window box can be a riot of colour.

Pots can provide instant colour.

Pots

A wide variety of pots and containers can brighten up a paved area by providing instant colour. This will be particularly useful in a new garden, while you are waiting for other planting to become established. Choose pots to complement one another and the house they adjoin; too many different types and styles brings confusion.

The range of pots is enormous, but where possible you should respect an underlying theme. Don't therefore, mix stone, terracotta, plastic and wood all together; it will look a mess. If there is a particularly strong architectural theme, capitalise on it. A classical Georgian façade will look fine with 'Versailles' tubs and bay trees on either side of the front door, as will a thatched cottage with old half-barrels filled with trailing geraniums. A crisp, modern building will be well suited to shiny plastic pots and annuals in primary colours.

Most homes, however, are not that precise, and a sensible choice of one or two types will do very well indeed. If choosing terracotta, which blends perfectly into most settings, make sure it is frost-proof – terracotta pots imported from abroad often are not.

When using groups, work in odd numbers. One is fine by itself, two is awkward, three good, and so on. Also vary the height and size to make a set piece rather than a clump all the same.

In many ways a pot should be incidental to the plant it contains; I have many broad-leafed plants such as hostas and trailing pelargoniums in a variety of buckets. In full summer, the containers are completely hidden. I also have a fine old cast-iron bath which is an ideal herb garden. Ample depth of soil and a built-in plug hole for drainage! It all comes back to the fact that we should always be looking for alternative uses for things. Railway sleepers make fine steps, baths make fine herb gardens and chimney pots make superb pots for planting. Whatever the container, make sure it is of ample size and of adequate depth; shallow pots dry out quickly and there is nothing worse than returning from a weekend away to find lifeless plants.

Some pots are, of course, quite superb in their own right, and these can stand alone, unfilled, as a piece of sculpture. Find a dramatic position for one; at the turn of a path, as a focal point at the end of a pergola or as the centrepiece of a formal composition.

Hanging baskets

While pots and containers look after 'instant colour' at ground level, hanging baskets can take us into the third dimension. A good basket is a sure sign of summer, but don't tackle the job before the end of May because late frosts can be a problem for half-hardy annuals until then.

Filling hanging baskets

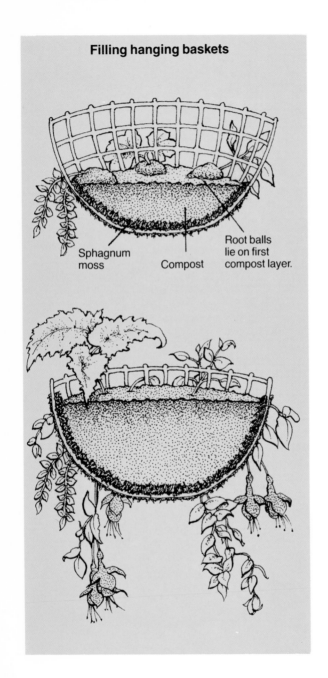

Sphagnum moss

Compost

Root balls lie on first compost layer.

Filling a hanging basket

Baskets come in a number of types: plastic bowls that incorporate a drip tray, simple galvanised baskets or perhaps best of all a plastic-coated wire basket that will give many seasons' service.

While compost can be placed directly into the plastic bowl type of basket, open mesh will need to be lined in some way. Sphagnum moss is available from most garden centres for this purpose, and looks far better than the black polythene which is the alternative. If using the latter, pierce the plastic around the bottom to allow drainage.

To fill the basket, first line the bottom with a 2.5 cm (1-inch) layer of damp sphagnum moss. Next position a layer of damp John Innes No. 2 compost and start to insert trailing plants around the edges by pushing these through the moss from the outside so that the root balls lie on top of the compost. Carry on adding moss at the sides and topping up with compost to cover the roots of the plants pushed through the holes in the basket. Plants should be positioned about 12.5 cm (5 inches) apart. Continue like this until the basket is full. If you are using polythene then you will have to slit it as you go to insert the plants.

Suitable trailing plants would include many half-hardy annuals such as the semi-pendulous buzy lizzie (impatiens), trailing lobelia, pendulous begonias, ivy-leaved pelargoniums (*Pelargonium peltatum* varieties), trailing fuchsia and 'Wandering Jew' *(Zebrina pendula)*. For the top of the basket use more upright plants such as verbena, petunias, ageratum or tagetes.

Place the basket in a sunny, sheltered place on a secure bracket, and be sure to water it twice a day in dry weather. Liquid feeding can be carried out every two weeks. Hanging baskets containing bulbs are less common but are in fact quite practical and make a delightful spring display.

Pools

Water can be one of the major elements of a garden and the way in which it is handled can make or mar a composition. One does not need a 'Geneva' fountain to make a statement, in fact a simple bubble jet that gives just a tinkle of sound and a ripple of movement is often far more effective, particularly on a hot summer's day. In fact, a high fountain in a small pool not only looks out of place but often empties the pond, because any slight breeze blows the water straight out!

As far as location is concerned, an open position is really essential as neither aquatic plants nor fish thrive in shade. Overhanging trees will drop leaves into the water, and this will lead to the build-up of toxic gases which could eventually kill the fish, particularly if the water becomes frozen over in the winter. If leaves are a problem – and they can certainly blow in from other areas

– cover the pool with a lightweight net during the autumn and remove this and the leaves together when the main fall is over.

Shape
The basic design rules for the shape of a pool are the same as those used elsewhere. This means that a formal or rectangular pond will look comfortable close to the house, probably set within or adjoining a paved area, while an informal pool, of 'free-form' shape, will look far more comfortable in the more distant reaches of a garden.

A pool in a terrace or patio can link into the paving pattern positively, being contained or emphasised by panels of brick or slabs. There might also be an opportunity to create split-level pools, one falling into the other. This could be particularly effective when there is a change of level, the pools interlocking with steps to form an interesting composition.

In an informal situation a stream can take advantage of the slope, and flow into a pool below.

Size and depth
A healthy pool is one that has a balance of aquatic plants, fish of different kinds, water snails and other life. Generally speaking, the smaller the pool the more difficult it is to achieve a balance, and, as a general rule, the minimum size is approximately 1.8 × 1.8 m (6 × 6 feet). Depth is another consideration: contrary to popular belief a maximum of 45 cm (18 inches) is quite adequate.

The cross-section, or 'profile' of the pool is important, however, and there should be a marginal shelf around at least half of the pool on which to stand plants that thrive in these conditions. The shelf should be 22 cm (9 inches) below the surface and about 30 cm (1 foot) wide.

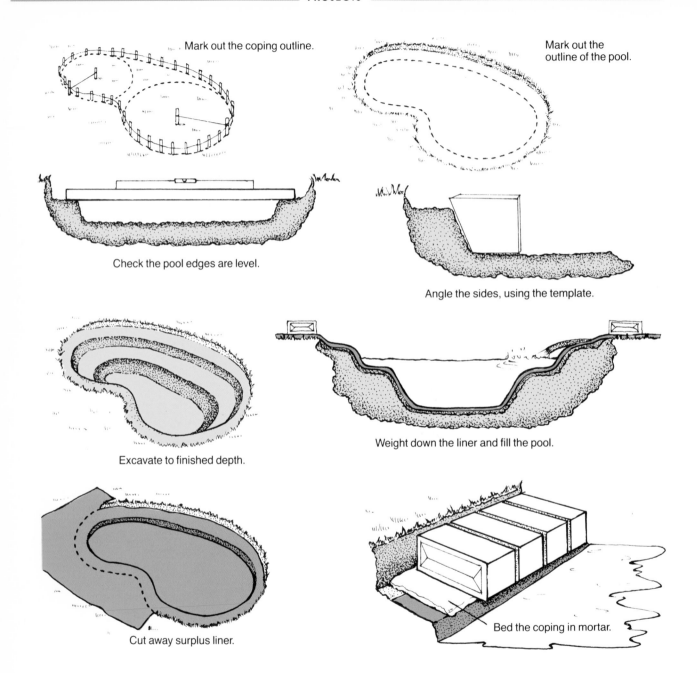

Mark out the coping outline.

Mark out the outline of the pool.

Check the pool edges are level.

Angle the sides, using the template.

Excavate to finished depth.

Weight down the liner and fill the pool.

Cut away surplus liner.

Bed the coping in mortar.

Constructing a pool

Up until about fifteen years ago, pools were built largely from concrete; although adequate, concrete pools always had problems with hair-line cracks and subsequent leaks, which were almost impossible to find. Construction was far from easy, and was time-consuming and expensive. Today the use of 'liners' made from varieties of PVC, rubber or polythene has revolutionised pool construction, which is now well within the capabilities of most home garden builders. Such liners are tough and durable, and if laid properly can last almost indefinitely.

As well as liners there are moulded, semi-rigid pools available, in fibre-glass or PVC. These are extremely easy to install but are limited in size and shape.

To build a pool using a liner you will need the following basic equipment: spade, shovel, pick-axe, plywood template angled at 20 degrees, long straight edge, spirit level, soft sand (with small particles that tend to make it 'sticky'), and, of course, the pool liner. Many garden centres will offer a liner for a set size of pool (taking into account the depth and marginal shelves) but if you want a larger size than is normally available just add twice the maximum depth of the pool to both the width and the length to give you a sheet of ample size.

Liners also come in all kinds of colours. The golden rule is to keep it simple; those with pebbles printed on the bottom look awful! Black is by far the best colour, because it increases surface reflections and virtually disguises the bottom altogether.

The illustration opposite shows pool construction and indicates a pool set in a flat lawn area. First mark out the shape of the pool and any coping around the edge, using a line swung from a cane set in the centre of the circles involved.

Carefully lift the turf with a sharp spade, stacking it carefully for use elsewhere in the garden. Next mark out the actual size of the pool, which will be inside the coping line already set out. Ensure that the edges of the pool are absolutely level by checking from side to side and end to end with a spirit level supported on a long straight board. Remove the soil to a depth of 22 cm (9 inches), using the template to achieve an angle of 20 degrees to the vertical. As the soil will almost certainly be fertile topsoil, stack it in a safe place. It could be useful for a raised bed or for backfilling behind a retaining wall. Once the shelves have been marked out, excavate the rest of the pool to the finished depth.

Remove any sharp stones that project from the bottom or sides. Then, using a trowel, spread a layer of damp sand on the bottom and sides, to act as a cushion for the liner. Place the liner over the excavation and weight the edges down with loosely laid coping stones. As you fill the pool with water the liner will be moulded to the shape of the excavation. Once the pool is full, trim off any surplus liner around the edges leaving a band of about 30 cm (1 foot). If the pool is a free-form shape, this edge will probably be puckered. Slit it where it will be covered by the coping so that it lies flat. Bed the coping in mortar: if the front edge overhangs the water by about 5 cm (2 inches) it will cast a shadow, disguising any glimpse of the liner below.

Semi-rigid pools

Fibreglass pools come in a number of different sizes and shapes and are generally stronger and more expensive than vacuum-formed PVC pools. Both kinds can be bedded on sand within suitable excavations; again check that they are absolutely level. As mentioned earlier, they are generally only available in rather small sizes, and this does

A pool is a welcome feature in any garden.

make it more difficult to establish a balanced pool environment.

Maintaining and stocking the pool

I have already said that a successful pool needs the correct balance of plant and aquatic life, and you will find that specialist garden centres sell collections of plants and fish suitable for a particular pool surface area. The pool will almost certainly go green after you first fill it, but this is quite normal and with correct stocking it will usually clear after about three months.

A pool does not need draining every year to clean it out — indeed, this will completely upset the balance so carefully set up. If you have a small pool, just remove about a quarter of the water once a year and replace it with fresh. Large pools should not need any draining. In summer, evaporation may be substantial, particularly if you have a stream that flows into the pool. If this is the case, keep a hose handy for topping it up.

Water used in other ways

There is always a fear, particularly when there are young children present, that a pool could cause a potentially fatal accident. However this need not by any means eliminate water from the garden. 'Millstone' fountains that are set at ground level or within a raised bed are becoming increasingly popular. The imitation fibreglass kind can be bought off the peg, but, inevitably, never look quite like the real thing. Use a solid piece of slate or a large smooth boulder drilled through the middle and set on brick piers within a tank. Place a submersible pump between the piers, fill the tank and water flows up through a pipe, through the central hole and back down into the tank again.

A treat for eyes and ears – a tiny millstone fountain (above). Constructing the fountain (below).

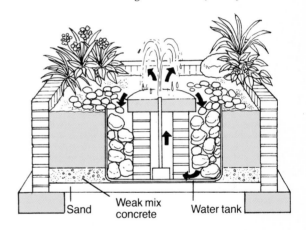

Sand   Weak mix concrete   Water tank

Paddling pools

In a hot summer a paddling pool can provide toddlers with hours of fun. The rigid PVC kind is cheap and easily moved around the garden to catch the sun or shade as necessary. For a more permanent feature, why not make a splash pool within a terrace? It need only be a few inches deep and can be floored with either 'brushed concrete' or very small cobbles (see pages 62–3 and 65–6). If you can fix up an overhead shower from an adjoining wall, happiness will be complete! (But remember *always* to supervise water play.)

Rock features

The 'currant bun' rockery, built of a myriad small pieces of stone, or worse, concrete, is an all-too-familiar site in many gardens. It is not only hard to maintain because of all the small pockets of soil, but also hard on the eye, because it is usually set on a poorly shaped mound that fails to blend with the rest of the garden.

To look its best, any feature using rock needs to be as natural as possible. This means that it hardly makes sense to use Westmorland stone in Somerset or Purbeck stone in Cumbria. Not only will these stones look out of place but they will be extremely expensive, owing to the long-distance haulage charges involved. Most parts of the country have a local stone which will blend perfectly into the local environment and local gardens.

It is also important to set the feature in a realistic manner. If you go out to a part of the country where rock outcrops naturally, you will probably see that the strata are set at an angle and that all the rock in the vicinity echoes this line. The same approach should be taken in the garden. Start with one large piece of stone and set this at a slight tilt, or 'bedding plane'. Match the angle with all the other stones in the group and remember that a good rock outcrop is rather similar to an iceberg, most of it is hidden below the surface!

As a general rule it is better to use a limited number of large stones rather than a mass of smaller ones. If you are in the position to hire a mechanical digger and purchase really substantial chunks of rock then you can look forward to a dramatic end-result. Whatever method you use to

A rock feature that looks in keeping will add drama in the garden.

set the rock, remember that even small pieces are heavy and two or more pairs of hands to help are sensible.

Rock outcrops look more comfortable in a sloping garden, where they can mimic the natural landscape. In a flat garden you will either have to import soil to build the levels up or perhaps create a large pool and use the excavated soil as the basis for the rockery, remembering to bury any subsoil beneath a 15 cm (6-inch) layer of rubble, topped with fertile topsoil. This latter should be 22–30 cm (9–12 inches) deep, and made up from a mixture of good quality topsoil, grit, leaf mould and peat.

When planting a rockery, consider creating a specialised environment. Many of the tiny but tough Alpine plants enjoy the sharp, free draining soil referred to above, and some of these will even grow in small stone chippings, mixed with soil, peat or leafmould and sharp sand, the latter being known as scree.

Herb gardens

Herbs have long been cultivated for their medicinal powers and culinary usefulness. They are not only one of the gardener's oldest and most useful friends but also extremely handsome, most having a delicious fragrance. Because of their use in

Laying a rockery

Put the first stone in at an angle.

Match subsequent stones to the same angle.

the kitchen it is practical to have a bed of herbs close to the back door.

The only possible disadvantage is the fact that most herbs are exceptionally strong growers and for this reason should be cultivated in pots or contained in some other way. Pots, half-barrels and buckets are ideal, and earlier in the chapter I mentioned my own collection, wallowing in an old bathtub — a perfect solution. An alternative, and one that can look particularly good in the architectural setting of a terrace close to the house, is the creation of a purpose-built garden using a geometric pattern. If the paved area is large, slabs can be removed in a chequer-board pattern, the gaps filled by herbs. Alternatively, raised beds at different levels can interlock with one another, with herbs tumbling from one level to the next. Another solution might be to build a 'herb wheel', the spokes of which could be brick or low hedges of box or lavender. The hub of the wheel could play host to a sundial or birdbath, the whole composition acting as a delightful focus.

Barbecues

There is only one thing better than using fresh herbs in the kitchen, and that is sprinkling them on a sizzling barbecue!

Meals outside have a flavour all their own, and barbecue equipment can either be bought off-the-peg or built into the garden framework as a permanent feature. The first option is usually cheaper and has the advantage that you can move it around the garden to follow the sun or to prevent smoke blowing in a particular direction. In a small house and garden it may, however, be difficult to find storage space for the winter months. To be honest, most portable barbecues are not large enough to cook a substantial meal for a group of friends all at one time.

Constructing a barbecue

For these reasons it may well be worth considering constructing a purpose-built barbecue that could fit into the design of a terrace, close to the kitchen, or perhaps another sitting area better situated to catch the evening sun. In the illustration opposite we show a sensible brick-built design that could incorporate both a built-in cupboard for storing tools and charcoal, and fixed seating. Some new houses are now being equipped with an outside gas point, specifically for barbecuing, while portable gas bottles are another alternative heat source.

Seats

Seats are generally furnishings and as such really put the finishing touches to a garden, something that we can discuss a little later on. Permanent

A seat can be a delightful focal point in a design. Site it to take advantage of a good view.

A pergola

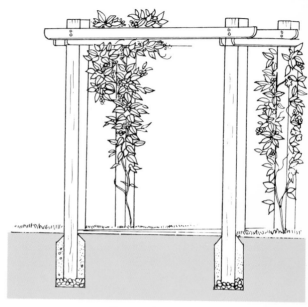

Constructing a pergola

seating is rather different however and can be built into the main structure of a garden. Sometimes it can take the form of raised bed, with a wide wall to one side, sometimes a retaining wall can serve much the same purpose. Large old trees can provide the perfect host to a sensible timber seat and you can buy off-the-peg patterns that are rectangular, circular or hexagonal. The home-built variety can be quite big, say 2.4 m (8 feet) square and can double as a sun-lounger, table and play surface. Children will find climbing on and jumping off this sort of platform great fun.

Pergolas

Many people get confused and call these pagodas, which are in fact Chinese or Indian temple buildings! These are hardly suitable for a domestic garden, although Kew has a beauty.

Pergolas are a series of archways, usually spanning a path or dividing different areas of the garden. They are very much a main structural element of the overall composition and to work in visual and practical terms they should have somewhere positive to go, leading both feet and eye in a particular direction.

Climbing plants can be trained over the structure and if well covered the pergola becomes almost incidental, simply a vehicle for the plant material. The latter will do far better in this sort of open position than if planted against a wall or house where it may be in a rain shadow or have poor soil conditions.

Construction should be simple and strong. Avoid 'rustic' timber straight from the tree, which tends to rot quickly. If you have the time, cash and ability, brick piers and stout timber beams look superb, but the garden will have to be large, to avoid looking pretentious.

Planting can add interest to an arch.

Constructing an overhead beam area

Most climbers are suitable for growing on pergolas, but don't mix more than two species together, because the whole composition becomes too fussy. Choose from roses and clematis, laburnum and wisteria and as a single species try that fine ornamental vine *Vitis coegnetiae* with huge rounded leaves that turn a glorious red in the autumn.

Arches

Arches are the doorways of your outside room; they focus a view and guide you through a particular opening. Like pergolas, make them simple and straightforward. Timber is the usual material for construction but there are some lovely old wrought-iron and wire versions, if you can get your hands on them. They are usually made from heavier gauge metal than their modern counterparts, which on the whole look feeble.

A solid arch can start life as a swing, with a temporary path leading around the side of it. Once the children grow up you can grow plants over it and redirect the path between the uprights.

The best way to support climbers on both pergolas and arches is to run wires through eyes up the supports and along the top, tying the climbers in as they grow.

Overhead beams

These are directly related to pergolas but where the latter are free-standing, overhead beams are attached to a house or garden wall. In town they are particularly useful to break the sight lines from neighbouring windows and when softened by climbers will also cast dappled shade. I normally build them from floor joists measuring 22 × 5 cm (9 × 2 inches), and support the end adjoining the house with galvanised joist hangers. The other end can be held by either a scaffold pole or square metal post; if using the former it can be fitted with a wooden dowel, a double-ended screw making the fixture. The

This arbour is a delightfully sheltered place to sit.

poles look best painted black while the beams can either be stained with a non-toxic preservative or painted to match the woodwork on the house. Incidentally it looks better to keep the ends of the beams square, as in the illustration above. Many builders and landscapers trim or 'nose' these off at an angle, but this simply looks fussy.

Arbours

These are really a combination of a pergola and a set of overhead beams, forming a free-standing canopy over a sitting area which is usually separate from the main patio close to the house. Mystery is one of the essential ingredients of good garden design and a secret garden including a rose-smothered arbour will be a delightful feature. The best arbours are simple in outline and usually open to the elements. Resist the temptation to cover them (or overhead beams) with clear plastic; it not only looks frightful but sounds like thunder when it rains. It is also difficult to remove leaves from the top and the surface usually goes green with algae; not a pretty sight!

This well positioned summer house creates a charming focal point.

Garden buildings

These can be broadly classified into utilitarian and decorative. The first category includes sheds, greenhouses, bin and bike stores, free-standing garages and workshops. Access will be a prime consideration and during the design stage you should have worked out the route of paths and positioning of any necessary hard-standing, making both of these generous enough for feet and barrows. There should be a parking and turning area outside sheds and greenhouses. The outline of all these buildings will probably be unattractive and there may well be a need for screening, either with planting or perhaps with a carefully positioned trellis clothed with climbers. A useful location for a shed can sometimes be that awkward dead passage at the side of a new house which hardly ever goes anywhere and remains in deep shade for most of the day.

Decorative buildings are altogether different, these are to be seen and as such can become an important focal point. Conservatories are becoming increasingly popular, providing useful additional living space and a delightful link between inside and outside, particularly with plants on both sides of the glass. If possible, try and match the style of conservatory to the architecture of the house. A Victorian pattern looks way out of place on a modern suburban semi, where a simple, less decorative pattern would look fine.

Summer-houses are free-standing buildings and come in a wide range of styles, from the ostentatious Austrian chalet type to ludicrous 'wild west' log cabins. The owners of these more often than not fill them with jacuzzis and exercise bikes, which fool the neighbours into thinking they are fitness fanatics. There are a number of sensible, low-key traditional designs that look fine, particularly when tucked into a sweeping border or below a group of trees. Like their utilitarian cousins, they will benefit from a well planned path and can be sited to catch the sun when this moves off the main terrace close to the house.

Play areas and equipment

When there are children in a family they usually make the garden their own — and quite rightly. This means that the composition should have been planned with ample paved area for play, paths for wheeled toys and lawn for ball games. I suspect my kids are pretty typical and we have a shed given over to bikes, swing tennis sets and toys of all kinds, which change as the children grow older. In other words storage is important, as is a wide path to reach it.

Fixed play equipment, and it must be well anchored, will normally include a swing and slide, although there are some impressive climbing frames and log castle affairs that take up rather more room. It can be both practical and attractive to children, who love seclusion, to house all this gear in a separate garden 'room', screened by a wing of planting or a hedge. If you are lucky enough to have some old fruit trees with rough grass below this will make an ideal play space, being harder wearing than a fine lawn.

As an alternative to grass you can surface the area beneath permanent play equipment with a thick layer of chipped bark, which is hard wearing and soft on the knees.

Tree houses are a possibility but should always be built with safety in mind, while Wendy houses are fun for the smaller ones. If you buy them off-the-peg you will probably want to screen them becaus, they can look pretty terrible! Play for the very young should be in full view, however, so a sandpit on the terrace, close to a kitchen window, will be ideal and easily swept up after use. The pit could be raised, in which case it can change use to a bed or pool later in life. Fit a wooden cover to double as a play surface and to discourage cats.

Children's gardens

Children's gardens are often talked about but are something of a misnomer as really the whole garden should be for children — and usually is! However, there is often a real need to set aside an area where children can have a go at growing things. They may need help from a grown-up, but will rarely welcome it, so guidance will need to be subtle and one should not be too worried if the whole project goes badly wrong or simply gets abandoned after a few days.

Many terrific plants can be grown, but children particularly like to see the fruits of their labours *quickly*. This being the case, try sunflowers; this is real Jack and the Beanstalk stuff! Sweet peas take a little longer and don't grow so big but are devastatingly pretty and smelly too — children love them. On the vegetable front, simple things like radishes and lettuces are good. You don't need a special area, use a spare patch in the front of a border. Then there is a natural and welcome interest in anything that flies or moves. They will be fascinated by butterflies and bees on sedum and buddleia, and this will give them an interest in the wider garden. September is the month of spiders, and garden spiders are truly beautiful. Show them to youngsters before they are indoctrinated with terror and they will have no fear of these magical creatures for the rest of their lives.

Water needs to be treated with respect and this should be taught as early as possible. My own daughter and a friend built an excellent pool and rockery in her early teens, planted it, stocked it and watched as tadpoles and frogs developed. After that there were dragon and damsel flies; when you see those colours for the first time you realise that nature beats us hands down. The pool involved little expense, because they used an off-cut of liner from our larger pond.

So don't relegate the kids to a miserable patch out of the way, that's how they will lose interest. Involve them in the whole concept and watch out, they may soon be telling you the best way to do things!

Lighting and power

Electricity in the garden can be an invaluable friend, but if used or installed incorrectly it can be an equally deadly enemy. Only install it if you are absolutely sure of your capabilities. Always follow wiring instructions to the letter, and if in any doubt call in a professional; his charges will probably be modest and well worth it.

Like garden buildings, lighting and power fall into the two basic categories of practical and decorative. On the growing front, electricity is needed to heat propagators, warm soil, drive irrigation systems and automatic vents and much more. It will power mowers and other tools, operate pumps for fountains and waterfalls and, of course, provide lighting. The latter will be primarily used for highlighting key areas and to provide a burglar deterrent in the immediate vicinity of the house.

The normal house voltage is usually stepped down to a safe level by a transformer, this being wired back to a separate fuse in the main fuse box. If you do take mains voltage down the garden, perhaps to a workshop or garage, consult an electrician and run armoured cable through a deeply buried heavy-duty plastic pipe.

In lighting terms, stick to that basic design rule: simplicity. A few well chosen and sensible fittings will be a world better than an imitation of the Blackpool illuminations. There will be two broad areas to consider: first those on or near the house and second the more distant parts of the garden.

House lighting
The range available is pretty ghastly and the prime rule is to respect the underlying architecture of the building. Pseudo-Victorian lamp posts and Georgian coach lights on or beside a between-the-wars semi would be, frankly, ludicrous, but in the real setting would look fine. There are a number of good, sensible low-key fittings available if you hunt them out. Remember that it is the light and not the holder that is the important thing.

At the rear of the house, a few well positioned lights will show the way around the building and can be carefully sited to illuminate a barbecue or outside sitting area. Steps are particularly important and there are a number of fittings that can be recessed into the risers or alternatively the brickwork to either side. This will cast light where it is needed, on your feet, and not, as so often, on the top of your head!

Garden lighting
Once you move away from the house, lighting should be used sparingly but well. A well chosen spotlight shining on a statue or urn and surrounded by bold foliage can be dramatic in the extreme. So too can a gentle pool of light on a group of shrubs.

What most people forget is the simple fact that we normally see plants illuminated from above by sunlight. If they are lit from below they take on completely different characteristics and the foliage has an entirely different pattern.

This kind of lighting is best set up by two people, one in the house, seeing the long-distance effect and directing operations, and one down the garden moving the light until it is in the right place. Such lights are normally set on ground spikes, although you can obtain fittings that will clip on to the branch of a tree to shine down.

The colour of bulbs is another factor to consider. Red, yellow and orange tend to turn foliage either pallid or downright sickly. Green tends to negate it altogether; blue and white are by far the most successful.

Pools
Lighting designed to be used underwater is quite safe, but do be careful to use it sparingly. There are a number of floating, rotating displays that are apt to bring on a migraine in record time! A gentle glow from below the surface can, however, be sheer magic.

Furniture

Like lighting and pots, the choice of garden furniture is limitless, so try and keep things simple and to a theme. Timber furniture is softer on the eye than plastic, but it needs regular oiling to keep it in good condition and prevent rot setting in. The hardwoods such as teak and iroko are best but they are expensive. Plastic can be excellent or tatty. At its best it has a crisp, modern look that can be teamed with bright fabrics and parasols. You need the latter on a bright day because the glare from a white plastic table is intolerable. Alternatively use a tablecloth and keep all the fabrics in the same colour, ideally teaming with a scheme inside an adjoining room.

Metal either comes in the traditional imitation wrought iron which looks fine, particularly outside a period house, or bent wire of different kinds. The latter usually looks flimsy and can be uncomfortable to sit on. Stone is also traditional and there are a number of well made seats and benches that can look fine in the right place, a formal garden, perhaps, or softened by foliage.

The use of benches is rather different to

Furniture should be chosen to match the style of the garden.

groups of furniture. Benches can be used as a focal point at the end of a path or on the other side of a lawn. They will draw the eye and have a useful role to play in design terms as well as their use for relaxation. Deck chairs seem, sadly, to have gone out of fashion, which is a pity as they are comfortable and great space savers when folded away. So too are 'director's chairs'. Both these and deck chairs are easy to cover in bright canvas fabrics or plastic woven material.

Hammocks are what a lazy summer afternoon is all about. They are easy to move around the garden to chase sun or shade, but do make sure they are securely fixed. Two stout branches are best and a degree of practice is needed to get in and out!

Statues and ornaments

These really are the finishing touches of a garden, and I never choose them for clients. This is because the selection is a personal one and reflects the owner's personality. Garden ornaments range from devastatingly expensive bronzes down to charming miniature pigs, or, dare I say it, gnomes. Now gnomes stir up hatred amongst horticultural snobs but if you really want one then why not? Humour is an essential part of gardens and garden design and a little fellow leaning on a rake by the pool is simply funny.

Siting a statue, or any ornament for that matter, is a tricky business because they are real focal points. Choose your place carefully and either make a dramatic statement by placing the item in full view or play it down a bit by providing a mantle of soft green foliage.

Of course not all ornaments are man-made. A well positioned smooth boulder can be a real eye-catcher, as the Japanese have known for many hundreds of years. So too will be an old

A well positioned statue can be a delightful focal point in a garden of any size.

fallen tree with a clematis or other climber running over it.

Topiary is living sculpture, and many plants can be trained or clipped into different ornamental shapes. The range of shapes is as wide as your imagination. Don't just think of animals, let your creativity loose a bit and remember: humour is your best friend.

MAINTENANCE AND MODIFICATION

To build a garden is an exciting and rewarding experience. It will have involved the whole family and should at the end of the day fit you all like a glove. Now that it is done, however, someone is going to have to look after it and unless you are one of the wealthy few who can afford a gardener then that person is going to be you!

If you have followed the guidelines set out in this book and gone about the design in a sensible and practical way, the amount of maintenance you plan to do should have been geared to the time and effort you can spare. A garden, though, is not quite like a room inside the house, even though we have gone about planning it in a similar way; it is a living entity and is consequently in a continual state of development. In broad terms, we can break down garden maintenance into the two areas of hard and soft landscape that have run as a theme throughout the planning process. Before we consider these two areas, however, it would be worth giving some thought to the tools needed for the jobs.

Tools

Tools are a bit like gardening books, it always amazes me just how many there are of them!

I have a fine garden and I also have a pretty basic range of tools which are as shown.

Spade   A spade is a supremely useful tool and has a wealth of uses, from the obvious one of digging to all kinds of mixing and shovelling operations. Spades come in different weights, lengths and types of shaft. You can have ordinary steel or the stainless variety; this costs a lot more but can make working heavy ground a good deal easier. When you buy a spade pick it up, feel it, try the balance and see if the handle is comfortable. I've never seen a garden centre with a patch of ground where you can try tools out, and this is a pity as it is the only real way to see if you like a spade or not. There are plenty of sports shops where you try out golf clubs or tennis rackets.

Once you have bought a spade, or any tool for that matter, keep it clean, sharp and lightly oiled with a light lubricating oil. It should then, quite literally, last several lifetimes.

Fork   I have a digging fork, which is great for turning over ground, breaking down soil, removing weeds and carrying them down to the compost heap. I also use it for prising apart herbaceous plants when I have lifted them, prior to replanting. A border fork is slightly smaller, a bit too small for my liking, but ideal for ladies or children.

Hand fork and trowel   These are a must for planting annuals and bulbs, or, in fact, anything small. The trowel does the digging and is also useful for filling pots and so on, while the fork breaks down the soil and removes weeds.

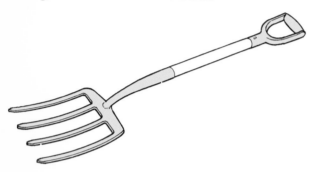

Rake   I don't have a border rake as I use a fork for spreading mulch and breaking down ground. I do have a lawn rake, however, which is terrific for scratching out ('scarifying') dead growth from the lawn, and also for collecting leaves.

Hoes   I have a Dutch hoe which is an invaluable tool. It is ideal for weeding in the border and also fine for scraping weeds from crevices in paths and so on. I also have a draw hoe which I use for creating seed drills. I also incidentally use it for mucking out my chicken houses: it's a great pity more people don't keep hens in their back yards!

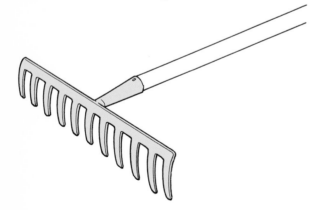

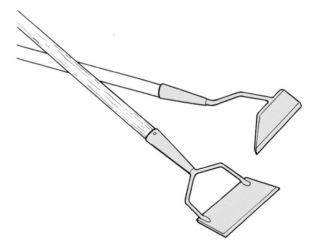

Shears I have an expensive pair of shears, which I keep as sharp and well set as possible. I use them for trimming shrubs and clipping hedges. I also have a pair of long-handled shears, which I use for edging the lawn. I far prefer these to the wealth of mechanical gadgets designed for the purpose. I must admit that I also prefer shears to the newly invented 'strimmer'. This is a useful tool, but to my mind you can do a lot of inadvertent damage with it, as it doesn't differentiate between weeds, long grass, bulbs and other planting, and a slip is easily made.

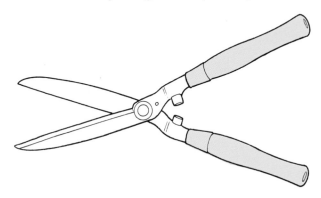

Secateurs This is my other indulgence and I have just about the most expensive secateurs that money can buy. Mind you, I have had them twenty years and never had them sharpened, and they still cut like a razor. This is absolutely vital when pruning, as a ragged cut is an invitation to disease to take hold.

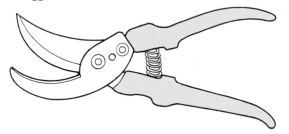

Pruning saw This too can be a murderous little weapon in the wrong hands. I find it invaluable for removing old, tough stems and for minor tree surgery.

Sickle My sickle is an old one but hones up to perfection. I use it for clearing rough grass areas, brambles and weeds. Sickles are, however, dangerous in the wrong hands. ALWAYS keep such a tool away from children.

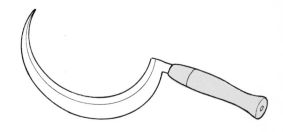

Wheelbarrow I have a large, straightforward barrow, with nothing fancy like a ball instead of a wheel at the front. I also have a sensible network of paths over which to move it.

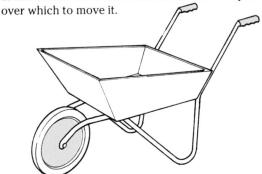

Mower   We discussed these on page 76. I have a small, hand-propelled machine, which is ideal for my small lawn. It is also far cheaper and almost certainly more reliable than the plethora of electric and petrol-driven types.

Apart from hand tools I have an excellent snap-together hose-pipe system, with all the attachments, an oscillating sprinkler and two watering cans, one kept solely for chemicals. I also have a cupboard in my shed to contain these chemicals. It is *always* padlocked.

Broom   The most important tool I have left to last! A good, long-handled stiff broom does more work in the garden than anything else — and it shows.

That is my tool set, and quite comprehensive enough for me. There are of course plenty more things you can buy and many of them will save you many hours' work. There is also an increasing range of tools for handicapped and elderly gardeners, who need lightweight handles, spring-loaded blades and other easy-to-use items.

Soft landscape maintenance

We have already considered the pruning of specific types of planting (pages 113–4), and this will remain constant for the life of the particular species involved. What will not remain constant, however, is the amount of general maintenance to keep borders in peak condition.

If we assume that the garden is planted with well grown but young material, it will follow that there are gaps between the various shrubs and hardy perennials. We have also seen that these gaps may be planted with annuals or ground-covering plants that will quickly knit together and help to eliminate weed growth.

Another way to keep down weeds is to spread a mulch of chipped bark. Bark mulch is becoming increasingly popular as a carpet beneath plants to exclude weeds and retain moisture. It comes in various grades, from large, rough chips 3–5 cm (1–2 inches) in diameter, which look a little coarse in a domestic garden, down to a much finer, granular mixture more akin to peat. While the latter looks attractive, it tends to work into the soil rather quickly, and you will be better off choosing a medium grade, with chips about 1 cm (½ inch) in diameter. Use a mulch of ample depth, at least 5 cm (2 inches), and top it up once a year to keep the beds looking immaculate.

However, all these approaches cost hard cash and there is absolutely no reason why you should not keep a newly planted area weed-free by the

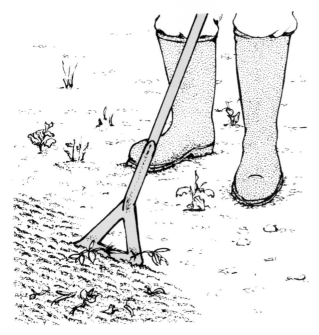

Walk backwards while using the hoe.

effective use of a hoe. This assumes that the borders were well dug prior to planting and all traces of perennial weeds were removed. To use a Dutch hoe properly is a satisfying business. Work it backwards and forwards just below ground level to sever weed roots. Be sure to carry out the operation on a regular basis and always before any weeds have had a chance to set seed. If you hoe regularly and encourage the new planting in those first few seasons by regular feeding and irrigation, you will be surprised just how quickly plants will knit together. Of course, as the plants grow, the gaps become fewer, and as the gaps become fewer, there is less room for weeds to grow. In other words, care of the general borders is very much on a sliding scale and the more effort you make in the early days then the greater the dividends in the longer term.

Lawns

Refer to the lawn-care calendar on pages 78–9 for the routine of lawn maintenance. There are other lawn problems that become apparent from time to time, however. Bare patches are one of these, and these can often be attributed to your own or a neighbour's bitch. Urine kills grass, but if caught soon enough can be sufficiently diluted with a bucket of water. Another cause of dead patches is buried objects, usually builder's rubble in a new garden. Peel back the turf with a spade, remove the soil and find the foreign body. Slightly overfill the hole with clean top soil and firm down, replacing with new turf or seed. The level will quickly return to normal as the ground settles.

The amount of weed-killing and the number of weeds you can tolerate is largely down to you. I can take quite a few! You can treat the lawn with a combined fertiliser and weed-killer and also a chemical 'spot weeder' on perennial species. There are also narrow trowels available that can neatly dig out a long-rooted weed.

Trees

A tree that has been carefully selected for the position in question and given the benefit of good growing conditions should present few maintenance problems. However, one often inherits trees that are not so healthy and the care of these is important. Dead branches should be removed for the obvious reasons of disease and the danger of a limb falling and doing damage below. If removing a limb, do so with two cuts, roping the branch securely to a sound limb above. The first cut will take the majority of the branch off, the second will remove the stub, avoiding the possibility of the whole branch ripping back the bark on the trunk.

Some trees are enormous and quite beyond the

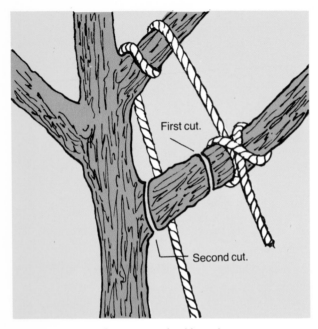

Removing a dead branch

scope of the average garden owner. If such a tree should need felling or thinning for any reason call in a qualified tree surgeon. He will advise you and his fee will be far less than the damage caused by a 500-ton tree falling in the wrong direction.

Remember, too, that certain trees in a district may be protected by law and it is always wise to contact the local council before taking any action.

Hard landscape

Paving
Paving on paths, patios and steps needs to be kept clean and free from slime, particularly in shady areas. You can use a weak solution of bleach and a stiff broom, but to be honest I am always wary of using bleach near plants. I tend to wash down any areas like this with a scrubbing brush and soapy water. It only needs doing once a year.

If paving is properly laid, you should rarely have any problems. Just occasionally, however, a stone gets cracked or a brick breaks down. If this happens, it is easy to trip up and have an accident. Remove the slab by breaking it into small pieces, or chop the brick out with a hammer and bolster (a special tool for this job). Clean out the area underneath, taking care not to disturb the surrounding paving, and replace the material involved on a bed of mortar, making sure the levels match exactly.

Timber
This can take the form of decking, fencing, sheds, summer-houses, arches, pergolas and overhead beams. In our temperate climate, rot sets in quickly, even if the timber has been pressure-treated before purchase; regular applications of a non-toxic preservative are essential. It is worth stressing again, however, that creosote should never be used in the vicinity of plants; it is a real killer.

If you are training climbers on any of these features, do so on wires that can be lowered to the ground, together with the plants, when maintenance is taking place.

A removable 'gravel board' (page 48) at the bottom of a fence will prolong the lives of panels or boards above, while concrete posts last a good deal longer than timber ones.

Walls
Walls, if new, should last many years without attention. Old brick walls that used the soft 'lime mortar' may well need repointing, however. If this is the case, the old mortar should be raked out to a depth of 15 mm (½ inch). Brush the wall down to

remove loose material, and damp down an area of about a square yard or metre at a time. Place a board at the bottom of the wall to catch the excess and use a mix of one part cement, six parts soft sand and one part plasticiser. Point in the vertical joints first and finish the work in one of the styles shown on page 44.

Modifying the garden

Although many people move home on a regular basis, there is an equal number who stay put for a considerable time. This being the case, a garden may go through several distinct phases, corresponding to changes in the life of the family.

The first of these is usually centred around the children, with ample room for play, the provision of a sandpit and areas where they can grow 'their own things'. After a while the priorities change, the sandpit becomes a pool or raised bed and the lawn is given over to the larger-scale games of cricket, football and badminton. Still later, the children leave and part of that lawn might be given over to the cunning and ferocious game of croquet or become a vegetable garden or even perhaps a small orchard.

Retirement brings greater leisure time, but also a slowing down; vegetables may give way to sweeps of low-maintenance shrubs and ground cover, while part of the lawn could become an extension of the terrace. If a garden has been planned correctly, with foresight, then such changes will be a logical progression rather than a total upheaval. A garden grows and matures, like we do. Treat it with respect and understanding and it will serve you with an ever-changing pattern of colour and pleasure.

Remember that, in the final analysis, a garden should be no more work than you want; it should serve you and bring you enjoyment, never the opposite.

INDEX